Watermelon Seeds

Stories, Thoughts and Ponderings of a Local Pastor
Considering the Seeds of the Faithful

*Based Upon the Parable of the Sower, Seed, and Soil
from the Glorious Gospel of Matthew 13:1–23*

Rev. C. Steven Melester

ISBN 978-1-63874-742-0 (paperback)
ISBN 978-1-63874-743-7 (digital)

Christian Faith Publishing, Inc.
832 Park Avenue
Meadville, PA 16335
www.christianfaithpublishing.com

Scripture quotations unless otherwise noted are taken from the Holy Bible, New International Version, NIV copyright 1973, 1978, 1984, 2011 by Tyndale House Publishers, Inc. and Zondervan Publishing House.

Printed in the United States of America

Contents

Preface

Anyone can count the seeds in an apple, but only God can count the apples in the seed.

—Robert Schuler[1]

That same day Jesus went out of the house and sat by the lake. Such large crowds gathered around him that he got into a boat and sat in it, while all the people stood on the shore. Then he told them many things in parables, saying: "A farmer went out to sow his seed. As he was scattering the seed, some fell along the path, and the birds came and ate it up. Some fell on rocky places, where it did not have much soil. It sprang up quickly because the soil was shallow. But when the sun came up, the plants were scorched, and they withered because they had no root. Other seed fell among thorns, which grew up and choked the plants. Still other seed fell on good soil, where it produced a crop a hundred, sixty or thirty times what was sown. Whoever has ears, let them hear." The disciples came to him and asked, "Why do you speak to the people in parables?" He replied, "Because the knowledge of the secrets of the kingdom of heaven has been given to you, but not to them. Whoever has will be given more, and they will have an abundance. Whoever does not have, even what they have will be taken from them. This is why I speak to them in parables. "Though seeing, they do not see; though hearing, they do not hear or understand. In them is fulfilled the prophecy of Isaiah: "You will be ever hearing but never understanding; you will be ever seeing but never perceiving. For this people's heart has become calloused; they hardly hear with their ears, and they have closed their eyes. Otherwise they might see with their eyes, hear with their ears, understand with their hearts and turn, and I would heal them." But blessed are your eyes because they see, and your ears because they hear. For truly I tell you, many prophets and righteous people longed to see what you see but did not see it, and to hear what you hear but did not hear it.

"Listen then to what the parable of the sower means: When anyone hears the message about the kingdom and does not understand it, the evil one comes and snatches away what was sown in their heart. This is the seed sown along the path. The seed falling on rocky ground refers to someone who hears the word and at once receives it with joy. But since they have no root, they last only a short time. When trouble or persecution comes because of the word, they quickly fall away. The seed falling among the thorns refers to someone who hears the word, but the worries of this life and the deceitfulness of wealth choke the word, making it unfruitful. But the seed falling on good soil refers to someone who hears the word and understands it. This is the one who produces a crop, yielding a hundred, sixty or thirty times what was sown. (Matthew 13:1–23)

In writing this book, I must share with you that I have no delusions of grandeur. In humility and gratitude, I simply offer these stories, experiences, eulogies, and ponderings in an attempt to give credit to those saints who have had a serendipitous part to play in my spiritual formation. Through sharing my stories and theirs, I hope to ignite in readers a discovery and appreciation for their own stories and especially for those people upon whose shoulders they stand.

This book is not a deep theological treatise or an exploration of John Wesley and Albert Outler's Quadrilateral.[2] This book is an attempt to open eyes, ears, minds, and hearts to the infinite possibilities for spiritual growth found in community through the many experiences and snapshots of life, and yes, of death. It is an attempt to embrace the mystery of our faith through the many ways God, through the Holy Spirit, births transformation. In all things and in all ways, I give glory, honor, and praise to my Lord and Savior Jesus Christ, who was, is, and always will be the master gardener. He is the vine and we are the branches.

Acknowledgments

I wish to thank all the saints and sinners, all those wonderful jars of clay that have helped me to become a better person, better pastor, and a more sincere follower of Christ. The people in this book are family, friends, colleagues, brothers and sisters in Christ, and fellow sojourners on the road of spiritual formation. They are as broken and human as I am, and they have shared with me their most intimate experiences of life and of death. I love them all very much and have been extremely blessed to have been a small part of their journey. I am thankful for the seeds they scattered my way!

I especially thank my soul mate and best friend of forty-eight years, my wife Melanie. We dated for five years, and she has still stayed married to me for forty-three years and counting! She is my rock of support, and "she is clothed with strength and dignity" (Proverbs 31:25). "Many women do noble things, but you surpass them all" (Proverbs 31:29). I am so blessed to have a partner in ministry that understands my deepest struggles and supports me with such devotion. God has bestowed upon my wife her own very special gifts and graces, yet she finds the time to always be there for me. I will always be eternally grateful for her patience with me; her compassion for our family; and her strong, constant, humble, and steadfast faith in God.

I am thankful for my family and especially for my two sons, Ben and Sam, who have always brought such joy to my heart. To my granddaughter, Abby, who is a bright light and constant source of delight. I am thankful for so many in my family who have contributed to my upbringing and growth as a person and as a Christian.

I am very humbled and very thankful for all those in my congregation who have nurtured me, challenged me, supported me, tolerated me, forgiven me, and loved me. To the congregation of Burnt Factory United Methodist Church, I am truly honored to be partners with you in serving our Lord. Your faithful generosity of spirit has strengthened me, encouraged me, and blessed me.

And finally, I am forever grateful to the people of Haiti, who have taught me so much about what genuine faith and hope looks like in the midst of great poverty, corruption, and challenges. The many Haitians I was blessed to come to know are people of abiding and deep faith. They are compassionate and very generous. They are a proud people who celebrate the gift of life with zeal and humility. They are thankful and gracious. They will always remind me that regardless of circumstances, joy is a choice! They will always remind me that love is the one, undeniable, and unifying ethos that connects all people, and they know that God is love!

"To God be the glory, for the things he has done."[1]

Introduction

So neither he who plants nor he
who waters is anything, but only
God, who makes things grow.

—1 Corinthians 3:7

In April of 2014, when on a mission trip to Haiti, one of the ministries I was charged with was delivering seed to the farmers of the area we were serving. I was given seventeen pounds of watermelon seeds that were found to grow exceptionally well in the Haitian soil. When it came time to disperse the seeds to the farmers, the local pastor, leaders of the community, and our mission team prayed over the seeds and asked God's blessing upon them. Well, there were more farmers that came that day than we anticipated, and because we didn't have enough seeds for everyone, it caused some tense moments and ill feelings. The three local farmers who were elected to manage the dispersal decided to break some of the eight-ounce bags down to four-ounce bags so that everyone could receive some seeds.

It was an unexpected surprise to see the overwhelming desire for seeds! I quickly came to understand that these meager seeds would make all the difference for feeding their families. In truth, it could be argued that these seeds could make the difference between life and death for these very poor subsistence farmers.

Even with the challenges we faced, the dispersal of these watermelon seeds became a great celebration for everyone who came received seeds and were thankful!

It was quite amazing, coming from the USA where the abundance of seeds and food are so taken for granted, to experience the unbridled exuberant response of these humble Haitian farmers upon receiving a few meager watermelon seeds. These seeds were life! These seeds were hope! These seeds would bring food to their families, stability to their personal economy, meaning and purpose to their toil! And you better believe that they had prepared their soil. They had plowed the way for the seeds to take root and be fruitful. I was humbled and inspired by their appreciation for the God-created, life-giving, wonderful mystery that is present in seeds!

In the parable of the sower, seed, and soil, Jesus is using well-known agricultural metaphors to teach valuable spiritual truths. How does this parable speak to us today?

Let me suggest that first, I believe that God is the sower of all good seed but perhaps also partners with us, enlists us, and enables and equips us to also farm for the kingdom. I submit that the sowers of God's word could include the saints of the church. They are the faithful who share the word of God, who give witness and testimony to God's love with humility. They proclaim, with confidence and fearlessness, the truth of Jesus Christ and the inerrancy of scripture. They are the teachers, preachers, missionaries, apostles, and disciples. They are the devoted, the committed, and yes, they are also the broken. They are also the sinners, the so-called unchurched, who have weathered life's storms and have overcome their infertile soil to find forgiveness, grace, and redemption in Jesus Christ!

All who partner with Jesus through the prevenient, justifying, and sanctifying grace of God to sow seeds and help cultivate soil are those who do God's will.

The seed is the word of God, both written and living, manifested in the Son Jesus Christ. It is the gospel, the good news! It is the truth of the grace of God—a grace that is spread across the land, the truth and grace of God that is scattered to every corner of the world and on every soil in hope of transformation, reconciliation, redemption, and salvation. It is what the kingdom of God on earth can be!

The soil, I will submit, is the reason for the parable, and represents the soul of all humanity. The soil is our heart, mind, and free will. It is our purpose, our meaning, our reason, or it is not. The choice is ours.

The soil is who we are but also who we can become. The soil is our plight, our circumstance, and our situation. The soil is our destiny, our legacy, and our wisdom. It is our life, and it is our future, and it is also our death. What kind of future and what kind of death is the question.

Jesus shares that there are four ways that after hearing and experiencing the truth of the seed that we respond! First, we must understand that God, in casting his amazing grace across all creation, is not concerned with efficiency as much as with generosity! I would argue that if this were about efficient use of the seed, it would not have been scattered in places that it would not grow. God is generous though and tasks the sowers with scattering his word anywhere and everywhere in the hope that, no matter the amount of difficulty, it will take root.

Let us not forget, that God is in the hope business! We can allow the evil one to steal the seed, we can allow our weak foundation to dismiss the seed, we can allow culture to corrupt the seed, or we can accept the seed and help others to accept the seed by preparing our soil and perhaps lending a hand in preparing theirs. Could this be considered kingdom building?

Oh, that all humanity would desire the good seed as much as those Haitian farmers! Oh, that God's children would yearn for the good seed of God's word to be planted in their hearts! Oh, that the children of God would do the hard work of preparing soil to receive the seed! Oh, that the Kingdom of God on earth could be realized through the seeds of truth.

"He who has ears, let them hear!"[1]

This book is about the many people who have come and gone in my life that have planted seeds in my soul and spirit. Many of those sowers are family, past and present. Many of those seeds have been passed down through the generations.

I have been the beneficiary of many sowers from all walks of life. They have been fellow church members, friends, colleagues, and yes, even an antagonist or two. These sowers have taught me, in almost every case, by both their words and actions. They have instilled in me many opportunities to grow as a Christian. They have challenged me to climb a little higher on the ladder of discipleship. They have instilled in me a desire to know more, do more, feel more, and to worship with genuine gratitude and awe!

The seeds they have helped God sow in my heart have made me realize, explore, and embrace the truth of the Gospel with zeal, gratitude, and humility. These many faithful believers have infused in me the need to do some cultivating. I have found myself, from time to time, digging up rocks and weeds from my soul. I have found myself, on occasion, tilling the hardness of my heart. A hardness that comes when, in my humanness bent for sinning, I take my eyes off Jesus Christ, my Lord.

I am thankful for the many sowers and cultivators who have enlightened me, convicted me, nurtured me, forgiven me, taught me, tolerated me, and loved me!

Those faithful Haitian farmers would sow more than watermelon seeds. They planted seeds of what humble gratitude and appreciation for God's providential care genuinely look like! They planted seeds of faith that were grounded by deep roots of hope and trust in God. These are seeds worth pondering!

"He has scattered abroad his gifts to the poor; his righteousness endures forever. Now he who supplies seed to the sower and bread for food will also supply and increase your store of seed and will enlarge the harvest of your righteousness" (2 Corinthians 9:9–10).

"Although the life of a person is in a land full of thorns and weeds, there is always a space in which the good seed can grow."[1]

PART 1

Fruit of the Spirit Seeds

But the fruit of the Spirit is love, joy,
peace, patience, kindness, goodness,
faithfulness, gentleness and self-control.
Against such things there is no law.

—Galatians 5: 22–23

I have learned that I really do have
discipline, self-control and patience but
they were given to me as a seed and it's
up to me to choose to develop them.[1]

—Joyce Meyer

Chapter 1

Seeds of Charity
David and Edna,
My Great-Grandparents

My mother was named after her maternal grandmother, and she did not just take on the name Edna but also inherited my great-grandmother's character. My mother was born in 1926 and grew up during the Great Depression. She was a proud member of what journalist Tom Brokaw coined, in his book of the same name, *The Greatest Generation.*[1] It was a time in our country's history when the majority of people lived in rural settings on small family farms. People were poor but proud. They worked hard and enjoyed the simple rewards of life found in nonmaterial blessings. They gained strength to persevere through the many challenges they faced by believing and embracing the threefold proven precept of God, country, and family. This precept sustained many a family through difficult times!

This greatest generation, strengthened by this precept, would later go off to fight a world war. They would, without hesitation, sacrifice everything to preserve a way of life that was near and dear to them. The entire country would pull together to defeat tyranny, no matter what the cost, because freedom was at stake. God, country, and family was at stake!

The war, for the United States, would begin in 1941. But for now, in 1936, my mother was a horseback-riding, farm-raised, book-loving, intelligent, beautiful ten-year-old girl who found great comfort and solace from the world in the bosom of her own mother's parents. My mother adored her maternal grandparents.

My mother loved Sundays, and yes, church was the center of the community. She enjoyed worshiping and attending Pleasant Valley Evangelical United Brethren Church, but the highlight of the Sabbath was going to her grandparents' house after services.

David and Edna had eleven children and twenty-seven grandchildren and loved every single one of them. They knew every birthday, and they made each one feel special. Their modest farmhouse was a gathering place where everyone was welcome, especially on Sunday afternoon. The table was always open to anyone who might drop by; and even in tough times, by living on a farm, they always seemed to have enough to eat and then some. My mother told me that it was true bliss to be there.

It was carefree time, a time of playing barefoot with her cousins, having plenty to eat, getting into mischief from time to time, and simply being together with extended family. She loved listening to the family stories, but the best thing of all was being loved on by her grandparents. My mother told me there was no better place to be on this earth than when she would climb up on her grandmother's quite luxurious lap and be engulfed in her loving arms as they rocked back and forth on the porch of that old humble farmhouse.

My great-grandparents didn't talk about charity, they practiced it! And they did so because it was natural to them. They did it without fanfare or applause. They did it because it was who they were. Their home was a gathering place, but it was also a safe harbor in the storm. It was a beacon of light and charity to those in need. Their generosity was no different from many families during that time period, but to my mother and many others, the charity of David and Edna went the extra mile.

After their children had been raised, their modest four-bedroom farmhouse became home to thirteen people. Thirteen people who had fallen on tough times, but that still required three meals a day. Here is the breakdown. David and Edna had their own bedroom. Two of the other bedrooms were inhabited by two of their sons, their wives, and their children. Alson and his wife Bee (Beulah) and their two children, Alson Jr. and Mary Ann, took the second bedroom. The third bedroom was taken by his son John and his wife Ada and their two children, Bobby and Mildred. The last bedroom was occupied by two of David's sisters and one of his brothers. The two spinsters, Aunt Mags and Aunt Sudie, had fallen on tough times and they had no place to go. Uncle Carson had sustained a brain injury and was extremely mentally limited. He could barely speak but did understand simple direction. Uncle Carson would sit by the kitchen stove most days and would help his sister-in-law gather wood or bring water in from the well. He, along with all who lived in that old farmhouse, had purpose and meaning in their lives. They were accepted and cherished. They had a home.

Everyone would chip in to help around the farm and to do the chores that needed to be done. David and Edna gave those who needed a roof over their head a home, not a house. This gave them back their dignity, for this act of charity was never a handout. It was simply the right thing to do!

When his son Alson died from bone cancer at a very young age, David and Edna, along with his widow, all helped to raise his children. These acts were not decisions to be made but innate and natural responses born out of Christian teaching. There was no thought or consideration given to any other options. Charity, modeled in radical hospitality and in Christian thought and practice, is the highest form of love, signifying the reciprocal love between God and humankind that is made manifest in the unselfish and sacrificial care of one's fellow human beings.

My great-grandmother was also a midwife and delivered hundreds of babies, seldom receiving adequate compensation but always the admiration and appreciation of a poor community.

I never knew my maternal grandmother, let alone her parents, but the seeds they planted in the history and heritage of my family tree have taken root in the generations since. What my mother learned from her mother and grandmother (chapter 9) has been passed down to me; and I have, in turn, passed them down to my sons and especially my granddaughter. Legacies need to be celebrated, talked about, and embraced. No matter what our family legacies are, good or bad, they help to make us who we are. We stand upon the shoulders of others, whether strong shoulders or weak. We learn from both.

Whatever our family history is—whether it molds us, strengthens us, tests us, teaches us, shames us, encourages us, loves us, or labels us—one way or the other, it is part of us. In my family, at least in part, I am thankful for a legacy of love and sacrifice. The legacy of charity and those who spread seeds of compassion and radical hospitality are perhaps seeds worth considering.

> If I speak in the tongues of men or of angels, but do not have love, I am only a resounding gong or a clanging cymbal. If I have the gift of prophecy and can fathom all mysteries and all knowledge, and if I have a faith that can move mountains, but do not have love, I am nothing. If I give all I possess to the poor and give over my body to hardship that I may boast, but do not have love, I gain nothing. Love is patient, love is kind. It does not envy, it does not boast, it is not proud. It does not dishonor others, it is not self-seeking, it is not easily angered, it keeps no record of wrongs. Love does not delight in evil but rejoices with the truth. It always protects, always trusts, always hopes, always perseveres. (1 Corinthians 13:1–7)

"When we give cheerfully and accept gratefully, everyone is blessed."[2]

"Carve your name on hearts, not tombstones. A legacy is etched into the minds of others and the stories they share about you."[3]

Chapter 2

Seeds of Joy
Sonny and Pat, Playing the Cards You're Dealt

Sonny and Pat were two of the first people I met when I arrived at my appointment to Burnt Factory United Methodist Church in the summer of 2006. Sonny served as treasurer; and Pat had served, at one time or another, in every position possible. Pat is a lifetime member of the church, having first attended before she was even born. Her family were the founding members of the church going back several generations.

Pat was a woman who was ahead of her time and in many ways, a pioneer. She was the first female lineman for the local telephone company, and she excelled at just about every sport she played. Unfortunately, there was no Title IX in her day. If she would have had the opportunities female athletes have today, there is no telling what she might have achieved. She was gifted at tennis and golf and in her youth, and she could play football with the boys in the afternoon and look beautiful for her high school prom that evening!

Pat never ran from a challenge or backed down from responsibility. Her family, including her extended family, processed a strong work ethic and a strong constitution. Pat's upbringing, which included the benefit of loving Christian parents and siblings, would serve her well in life. This would become evident, just ten years into her marriage to Sonny. While they were building their dream house, Sonny experienced a terrible, life-threating, freak accident which left him paralyzed from his midchest down. Pat's love for her husband never waned, and her care for him was beyond amazing.

Sonny had been a tall, robust, and strong man's man. He loved to hunt, he was a skilled trap shooter, and he worked hard and prided himself in being able to take care of himself. But in the prime of his life, at the age of thirty-one, he was confined to a wheelchair for the rest of his life. When Sonny shared his story with me, he said, "Steve, you just have to play the cards you were dealt. And to tell you the truth, I'm glad it happened to me and not my best friend, who was standing right beside me that day."

Sonny never blamed God and never stopped living life to the fullest. He was accomplished in many areas of life and kept working right up to his retirement. He responded to the devastation of his physical body with astounding positivity, and Pat responded with incredible perseverance. They never missed a Sunday service and were the epitome of a couple who took their marriage vows seriously. Especially the one that said, "In sickness and health."[1]

Pat became a nurse to Sonny's many needs over the years: needs that included wound care, helping Sonny through a leg amputation brought on by his diabetes, and simply being there for him till the day he took his final breath. The eulogy I gave at Sonny's funeral, I hope, will reveal the nature and character of this man, who "played the cards he was dealt."

Service of death and resurrection delivered on November 9, 2016

Not too long after I came to Burnt Factory to serve as their pastor, a group of around twelve people from the church was invited to a brunch in Shepherdstown, West Virginia, about forty-five minutes away. It was a fancy place! I didn't know Sonny very well at this point, but I considered it a genuine honor to be the one that was given the task of pushing him from the parking lot up the hill to the restaurant. I had never pushed him in his wheelchair before and to tell you the truth, I was a little nervous. I admired this man but also knew he could be a little cantankerous now and then. Well okay, he could be very cantankerous!

Anyway, everyone went on ahead, they were all in the restaurant before I got Sonny halfway up the hill. I was having a little trouble navigating through some gravel. He was patient and told me to keep on trucking. Well, just about the time I made it to a flat, smooth surface, just about the time, I thought, I've got this, the right-side wheel of his wheelchair fell off! I mean it just fell off! My first test as a wheelchair driver, as someone who was, in a certain way, carrying him along, just failed. I blew it! He almost fell over, but I was able to shift to the side a little and keep him upright. I didn't want to yell for help because I didn't want to embarrass him. And me! I didn't know at the time, that Sonny could not be embarrassed. That word wasn't in his vocabulary.

Well, he didn't even blink an eye. He said, "that's happened before, don't worry about it, just get me back to the van, I know what it is, we need to go buy a bolt." He even knew where the local hardware store was. Well I struggled to roll him on one wheel but I did manage to get him back to the van and prop him over until I could temporarily put the wheel back in place. He told me where to drive and sure enough, we found the hardware store, retrieved a new bolt, installed it, and before you know it, we were back at the brunch and had only missed the salad course!

I learned that day, that Sonny was a person who did not look at life as a series of problems or challenges or embarrassments, but that he looked at life as a series of opportunities to find solutions and overcome.

From the very beginning, he looked at his accident as a series of opportunities. He looked at life and at his accident as just another broken wheel that needed fixing. Sonny's mantra was "You have got to play the hand you are dealt." So, you can choose to moan and groan and complain about the wheels of your life falling off or about missing the salad course or about being paralyzed. You can choose to be upset at having to deal with what most people would have considered an embarrassing moment; or you can get on with finding a solution. The meal is not finished because you missed the salad.

If Sonny had lived in Jesus' day, he might have been the paralytic in the Gospel story found in Mark 2:1–12. The author shares about four friends and their paralytic comrade. These four friends wanted to carry their comrade to Jesus with the hope of receiving a healing. They encountered a crowd that was so big, they could not get their friend to where the great healer was sitting. They decided to carry the paralytic up unto the roof on the mat upon which he was laying. They proceeded to cut a hole in the roof which allowed these faithful friends to lower their buddy directly in front of Jesus.2 The mat represents Sonny's wheelchair and it was a great honor to be counted as one of Sonny's carriers and friend.

Many from the medical community have carried Sonny, many from the home health professions have carried Sonny, many friends and family have carried Sonny, neighbors and church members have carried Sonny and of course Pat has carried Sonny! And I want to say a word about Pat, talk about marriage vows being kept, talk about love being a verb, talk about commitment and devotion, talk about "In sickness and in health," talk about a love manifested in sacrifice, talk about strength and endurance and perseverance; talk about all of these virtues, all of these qualities and you would be talking about Pat! Yes, Pat carried Sonny! She would have been one of those four who carried him up on the roof so that he might have a chance at being healed.

Jesus saw the faith of the four friends and he said to the paralytic, "Son, your sins are forgiven" Mark 2:5 and to make the point of his great love and of his authority even clearer he says to the paralytic "Get up, pick up your old wheel chair and throw it away. Get up and go home." All of us that had the honor of being one of Sonny's friends have been blessed, all of us who have carried Sonny have been privileged! But the truth beloved, the irony sisters and brothers, is that we are the ones who have been carried!

Sonny is the one who by his attitude, his perseverance, his endurance, his indomitable spirit, has carried all of us! His tremendous drive and fortitude, his unrelenting, and downright stubborn will power, his "get it done" mantra, his striving for perfection and excellence in all that he did, has carried us! His willingness to go the extra mile for anyone who had need, his facing terrible odds with a positive outlook, his fighting the good fight and running the good race, his unbelievable will and tenacity to overcome, has carried us! His love for his wife, his family, his country, his church and for his Lord, has carried us! His faith, his integrity, his dignity, and his humor has carried us! Oh, yes, friends, we may have thought we were carrying him but he was carrying us!

From day one, Sonny and I became friends and he had my back. As a new preacher, coming into pastoral ministry late in life, I needed support and encouragement and someone to carry me, look after me, and defend me. Sonny and Pat did all those things. When I graduated from Wesley Seminary Course of Study School in 2010, Sonny and Pat and many of the members of the church came to my graduation, but Sonny was first in line when I stepped off the stage. He was the first to shake my hand and even though he would not admit it, I saw tears in his eyes.

Sonny was in my corner and I knew I could trust him and I will miss that. I will miss his wisdom and his advice. I will miss his example of what it means to suffer with dignity and I will miss his finding such joy in the little things we all take for granted.

Sonny carried me many times and in many ways and make no mistake about this; once you cut through the rough exterior, once you understood that his bark was worse than his bite, once you gained his respect by giving it back to him as good as he gave it; you found a man with a heart of gold and a man whose faith ran deep.

As Sonny's death was imminent and as he was struggling with the difficult effects of an unrelenting infection; he did have moments of clarity. It was during one of those moments, when it was just the two of us in his hospital room, that he looked at me and asked, "Is He calling me home?" I said, "I love you my friend and I will talk to you straight. You have fought the good fight; you have finished the race and you have kept the faith and now you have in store for you the crown of righteousness."

2nd Timothy 4:7–8

He said, he did not want to leave Pat. I assured him that she would be alright, that many people love her.

The next day, others close to him also comforted him and helped him to find peace and rest with God. Within a short amount of time, after coming to terms with his destiny, he did find peace and he did something that he has not done since that fateful day when that tree limb fell and changed his life; he surrendered. He didn't give up, he gave in. He gave in and embraced the promises of God and he claimed that crown of righteousness. He died in peace and without fear. He died with dignity and with integrity just as he lived.

"He said to the paralytic, I tell you, get up, take your mat and go home. He got up, took his mat and walked out in full view of them all. This amazed everyone and they praised God, saying, we have never seen anything like this." Mark 2:10–12

Friends, I had never met anyone like Sonny and I never will again. I want to assure you today; Sonny has gotten up; he has thrown that wheelchair away, and he has gone home!

Sonny and Pat lived their life together in joy. Their marriage was not perfect, but their home was always open. Their lives were an open book, encapsulating the good and bad parts. They loved life, loved their church, loved each other, and loved the Lord. They were generous and lived their lives together with blessed assurance of the truth of the gospel. Sonny and Pat played the cards they were dealt in this life with joy and blessed assurance of God's abiding grace and mercy. They planted seeds of perseverance, character, faith, and joy.

Perhaps these are seeds worth considering!

"Consider it pure joy, my brothers, whenever you face trials of many kinds, because you know that the testing of your faith develops perseverance. Perseverance must finish its work so that you may be mature and complete, not lacking anything" (James 1:2–4).

"It is a natural human inclination to think that living through trials and negative circumstances would not be an occasion for joy. Choosing to respond to life's difficult situations with inner contentment and satisfaction doesn't seem to make sense. Joy is a choice! But the Lord is the originator of true joy."[2]

Chapter 3

Seeds of Patience
Clyde—My Father,
Friend and Mentor

One of the most endearing qualities of my father was his patience. Dad was a self-employed HVAC contractor that took great pride in customer service. It was a small company made up of my dad; a bookkeeper, who was my mother; and me. It was a small-town business where a handshake was all the contract you needed. My father had the keys to half of his customers' homes in the glove box of his service truck and knew where the other half kept their keys. Our customers trusted my father!

In 1970, when I was twelve years old, I began filling my summers by tagging along with my father on service calls. I always liked working with tools, and I didn't mind getting dirty. I loved tinkering on my bicycle and exploring how to fix things, so it was a good fit to become my dad's helper. I learned a valuable trade that would serve me well for many years, but what I learned most from my father was how to treat people!

Dad treated customers like friends, and he never turned down hospitality. Many of our customers were elderly and lonely. They appreciated the service we provided but also cherished the opportunity to visit. It did not matter how busy we were or how behind in our daily schedule of service calls we were. If a customer invited us to have a cup of coffee, Dad never turned them down. He knew it was more than just a cup of coffee.

I would become so agitated with him as he just sat there around the kitchen table talking to this couple who had been married sixty years. They poured coffee, brought out the lemon cookies, and talked about the old days. Outwardly, I was putting on a good face; but I was dying inside because we had places to go, customers to see, and besides, I wanted to get done early so I could do what I wanted to do! But there we sat, listening to tales from the past, hearing about their latest medical issues, and simply wasting time!

When Dad finally ate the last cookie and gulped down the last sip of coffee, we headed for the truck. I could tell that Dad was agitated with me. He didn't scold me for my obvious rudeness, nor did he give me a dressing down. He simply looked at me and said that we will never put work ahead of people. He said many of our customers need more than their furnace cleaned and air-conditioner fixed. They need a kind friend who will listen!

Years later, after Dad had died, I was exposing my young son to the business I had taken over from my father. I found myself in the kitchen of yet another elderly couple eating cookies, sipping coffee, and listening. My son was waiting in the truck, itching to get going to the next job. The famous Yogi Berra quote resonated in my heart, "It's like Deja vu all over again!"[1]

As I climbed back into the truck, I remembered my dad's words, but more important than that, I remembered his patience. The work would always get done, the work would always be there; but the opportunity to allow people the dignity of sharing, the opportunity to prioritize people over profit, the opportunity to give people the greatest gift of all, may be a one-time moment we ignore at our own peril. One of the greatest gifts we can give anyone is to patiently listen as we offer our time.

It is a seed worth considering!

"Patience is better than pride" (Ecclesiastes 7:8).

"There is no love of God without patience, and no patience without lowliness and sweetness of spirit."[2]

"Let us not become weary in doing good, for at the proper time we will reap a harvest if we do not give up. Therefore, as we have opportunity, let us do good to all people" (Galatians 6:9–10).

"Too often we underestimate the power of a touch, a smile, a kind word, a listening ear, an honest compliment, or the smallest act of caring, all of which have the potential to turn a life around."[3]

Chapter 4

Seeds of Faith
Jane, "I Need a Church to Die In."

Jane was one of those people who just exuded positivity. She was almost aggravating with her constant joy. She was a Christian who lived her life with gusto and appreciation for all the wonderful blessings of God.

She was spiritual but not sanctimonious. She was the kind of person that people wanted to be around. She loved a party, she loved her family, she loved a cold beer, she loved working with youth at church, and she loved Jesus! She had a light that could not be ignored or dimmed. Jane had a deep and genuine compassion for people and was granted the spiritual gift of mercy. It makes sense that Jane would become a nurse. She used her gifts and graces with the area hospice ministry and also specialized in wound care. Jane absolutely reflected the glory of God that was within her.

Jane and I attended the same church for many years, but when I answered the call to become a pastor, I was appointed to another church. We went our separate ways and lost touch. It wasn't until years later when my wife Melanie ran into Jane's husband, Dick, at the grocery store that our relationship would be rekindled. Dick needed to talk, and the cereal aisle at Martin's Grocery store seemed as good a place as any. Dick shared that Jane had been diagnosed with colon cancer and the prognosis was not favorable. He said, she had received a death sentence. He cried as he shared the agony of watching the woman he loved suffer.

Melanie provided the same wonderful listening ear that she always grants to me. Dick was hurting! Their life, their family, their sense of security, had taken a giant U-turn. When their conversation ended, Melanie shared how very sorry she was to hear this news, gave Dick a huge hug, and offered my services as a pastor.

When Melanie got home, she was exhausted from the outpouring of raw emotion she had just experienced. She shared with me her encounter, and we prayed for Jane's healing and for this wonderful family's strength for their journey. I personally prayed that if she needed a church, an old friend, or a pastor, that she would walk through the doors of my faith community. That was my specific and intentional prayer!

Well, friends, that prayer was answered, and just a month after the grocery store meeting, I would have the great honor and privilege of reconnecting with Jane and her family and traveling with them on their difficult journey.

After Jane attended her first worship service at Burnt Factory UMC, she waited around for everyone to leave. I couldn't wait to hug her and talk and pray together. I never will forget what she shared with me. "Steve, you have a wonderful church. Everyone has welcomed us so kindly. I already know, this is where I want to be. I need a church to die in."

You know, sometimes it's a curse to be a nurse, for they know too much! Following are some excerpts from the meditation I shared at Jane's service of death and resurrection. It reveals the great quality of the seeds that Jane sowed.

Service of death and resurrection: eulogy delivered on December 15, 2011

In the 11th chapter of the Gospel of John there is a story about the death of one of Jesus' best friends. Jesus spent a lot of time at the home of a man named Lazarus; along with his sisters

Mary and Martha, and there is a good bit of biblical material that leads one to think that Jesus was, indeed, good friends with this family.

Well, Jesus received news that his good friend Lazarus was sick and he was summoned to come immediately, but Jesus didn't make it there for four days and his friend Lazarus died. Upon seeing Jesus arrive four days late; Martha runs to him and says, "Lord, if you had been here, my brother would not have died. But I know that even now God will give you whatever you ask." Jesus said to her, "Your brother will rise again." Martha, said, "I know he will rise again in the resurrection at the last day." Jesus said to her and he says to us, "I am the resurrection and the life. Those who believe in me will love, even though they die, and whoever lives and believes in me will never die. Do you believe this?" Martha said, "Yes, Lord, I believe that you are the Christ, the Son of God, who has come into the world." John 11:21–27

Well, I must admit that I really didn't think this day would come. If I am being totally honest with you, I believed, deep in my heart, that somehow, some way, by some miracle, by some turn of events by some serendipitous event of some kind, that Jane would defeat this assault against her body; would somehow defeat cancer. There is no way, no how, by any stretch of the imagination that God was going to call home to heaven this spirit, this soul, this force, this dynamo of compassion and hospitality that was known as Jane! If anyone was going to beat the cancer that had so insidiously infiltrated her body, it was going to be Jane!

When the realization came that she was going to go home to be with the Lord; I understood that she had already defeated cancer. It didn't have a chance against Jane. Cancer didn't defeat her. She won the fight. I realized that it never did overtake her, for like Lazarus's sister Martha; Jane believed that Jesus is the Christ, the Messiah and that Jesus is the resurrection and the life! Death had already been destroyed by the power of the resurrection! Jane believed, as Martha, that even though we die, yet we will live again!

Cancer never won! Cancer never defeated Jane! Jane's earthly body may have succumbed to this disease but as Pastor Chuck Swindoll so eloquently shared, "Cancer never crippled Jane's ability to love or be loved. Cancer never corroded her faith or was able to eat away at her peace. It did not destroy her confidence and it did not kill friendships. It could not shut out memories or silence courage or invade her soul! And most assuredly cancer never quenched her spirit or lessoned the power of the resurrection!"[1] Through Jane's faith, courage, and spirit; cancer could never defeat her!

There were many times when visiting Jane that her faith and courage were evident. I thought I would try and cheer her up, only to realize that she was the one cheering me up. Her spirit was unique and her love for all aspects of life was inspiring! Her humbleness did not allow for her to consider just how many lives she touched and made better.

The frank discussions we shared, even upon her death bed, and the courage and faithfulness she bestowed will serve me all the days of my life. Her spirit, honesty, and integrity in the face of suffering and death has allowed me to grow as a pastor and as a person and I will always be eternally grateful. She taught me what genuine faith is and she taught me how to die with dignity! The prayer we shared together as she barely had enough energy left to speak will be forever a reminder of the power of the Holy Spirit and of a life that was grounded in love, sanctified in grace, and lived in hope!

Jane's one request of me for her service was to offer the path to salvation to those who may not know Jesus Christ. Her one request was for me to issue the invitation to any and all who may be seeking another way to live. She asked me to share that the grace and love of Jesus Christ is available to all and that the love of God is unconditional! She wanted me to make sure those present at her funeral heard the Good News, that there is nothing we can do that will make God love us less! Jane was still sowing seeds!

The truth in this story from John's Gospel is that just as Lazarus was freed from the tomb. Just as Lazarus was freed from death; just as Lazarus was untied and set free, so Jane has been untied and set free, not resuscitated, but resurrected!

The first words Dick spoke to me at Jane's passing, as we held vigil, was that she is now free! Jane has been loosed from her earthly body and is now made new again and is living in paradise, in God's keeping, where there will be eternal peace and serenity. No more tears, no more sorrow, no more pain, no more suffering. Jane believed in the promises of God and in the blessed assurance of Jesus Christ who said that "He was the way the truth and the life; who said he was going on ahead to prepare a place for us and if he went to prepare a place he would come back and take us so that where he was we would be also, for in my Father's house, Jesus says, there are many dwelling places.[2] John 14:1–6

Jane's faith was not a hollow crutch to help her get through life and death. It was not a token exercise to help her make sense of why we are here. Jane's faith was genuine, authentic, and strong! She knew that Jesus was waiting for her and it was her dream and desire that someone, even at her going home service, may come to accept the Lord Jesus as their savior and experience the peace of Christ; the peace that has sustained her!

Jane didn't like what happened to her; she didn't understand it all. Jane didn't cherish leaving her friends, her family, especially her two children; but Jane understood that God was still God and she still trusted God; still believed in God's amazing grace! The last words she expressed to me on her death bed, as I pressed my cheek against hers to try and hear her very quiet voice, was that everything was alright.

Maybe, a person's life when everything is stripped away is whittled down to one thing! Do we trust God? Are we faithful to his promises? It is seed worth considering.

"Because of the Lord's great love we are not consumed, for his compassions never fail. They are new every morning; great is your faithfulness. I say to myself; The Lord is my portion; therefore I will wait for him. The Lord is good to those whose hope is in him, to the one who seeks him" (Lamentations 3:22–25).

"Cancer is so limited... It cannot cripple love. It cannot shatter hope. It cannot corrode faith. It cannot eat away peace. It cannot destroy confidence. It cannot kill friendship. It cannot shut out memories. It cannot silence courage. It cannot reduce eternal life. It cannot quench the Spirit."[3]

"We continually remember before our God and Father your work produced by faith, your labor prompted by love, and your endurance inspired by hope in our Lord Jesus Christ" (1 Thessalonians 1:3).

"Those who know your name will trust in you, for you, Lord, have never forsaken those who seek you" (Psalm 9:10).

Chapter 5

Seeds of Kindness
My Compassionate Dad,
One Last Drink

My father grew up in severe poverty during the Great Depression. He knew what it was to go hungry. He knew what it was to serve in World War II and send your pay home for your family's survival. He knew what it was like to be shamed for being an uneducated country boy. He knew what it was like to drop out of school in the sixth grade to work in the orchards because his father was in jail.

Having said this, my dad had parents who loved him very much, but his father's alcoholism was problematic to say the least. My grandfather, whom I never knew, was not a mean or abusive inebriate but as my mother tells it was a quite happy and humorous drunk. He worked as a mechanic and part-time moonshiner. The problem was he sampled more than he sold! He was never abusive or mean but was a victim of the way he was raised.

My paternal grandfather, Elmer, was orphaned at six years old. He was farmed out to extended family who not only made it clear that he was not welcomed but also abused him. Perhaps this is why my father had compassion for alcoholics. He didn't excuse my grandfather's behavior, and when he would show up drunk around us kids, Dad and mom would shield us from his influence. I believe my dad wrestled with two very different emotions involving his father. He genuinely loved his dad and at the same time was inwardly ashamed. I believe he experienced simultaneously both respect and disgust but never hated his father and never judged him either.

Maybe this is what drove my father's choice one hot summer day when we were working at the home of a long-time, loyal customer who was battling terminal cancer. When we got to the house, his wife welcomed us and opened up the basement door. She said her husband was sick and didn't have long to live, but he wanted to see us before we left. She said she was going out to run some errands and when we finished servicing the furnace just go on upstairs and her husband would be in the living room in a hospital bed.

Sure enough, we found him just as his wife had said. He told us he was glad to see us and thanked my dad for his friendship and trusted service over the years. He said he didn't have long; the doctors said maybe a week. And then he grabbed Dad's hand, looked him square in the eyes, and asked him for a favor. Dad answered, "What can I do for you?"

The customer said, "They won't let me have anything to drink, and I sure could use a little gin. Could you see your way to get me a pint? I'm eighty-two, dying, and just want one last drink."

In today's world, this would be called enabling. This would be considered giving in to manipulation. This would be defined perhaps as being codependent. In any case, I believe by all accounts that the majority of people would have turned down his request and rightly so. Was my father's decision to go and get him a pint of gin and give him a couple of drinks an act of kindness or a grave mistake? There is a myriad of reasons that would support denial of this request, but Dad didn't see it that way. I'll let you be the judge, but to me, I saw an act of mercy and kindness given to a man who had made peace with his maker and was not long for this world.

Was it a bad idea medically? Was it morally wrong? Was it a weak moment for my dad? Did he give in as he had done many times for his own father? I'm not sure. To me, my dad's act that hot summer day was a kind thing to do. One of the greatest acts of kindness is to act with compassion beyond the given standard.

Perhaps it's a seed worth considering!

"Be kind and compassionate to one another, forgiving each other, just as in Christ, God forgave you" (Ephesians 4:32).

"For we do not have a high priest who is unable to empathize with our weaknesses" (Hebrews 4:15).

"Three things in human life are important: the first is to be kind. The second is to be kind. And the third is to be kind. Everything else is commentary."[1]

Chapter 6

Seeds of Goodness
Jay and Harriett, Haiti and Safe Harbors

In 2010, when I stepped off the plane in the poorest country in the western hemisphere, the first thing that hit me—I mean smacked me right in the face—was the heat and the smell. The heat in late August in Haiti is overwhelming. It saps your energy and creates in most people coming from affluence a feeling of anxiety. I think this occurs because the heat, which one can never truly escape especially in summertime, demands a different pace.

The hectic pace of Americans cannot endure in Haiti or any third-world country. One must embrace a kinder, much gentler pace to life to be able to be successful in Haiti. It takes a while to adapt, but I did. And through this adaptation to a slower pace, I came to appreciate many things we took for granted. I found a new appreciation for the simple refreshment found in a shade tree or a drink of cool water. I relished a shower that consisted of pouring rainwater, which had been collected in a fifty-five-gallon drum, over my body with a half-gallon bucket. I enjoyed the simplicity of a minimally cooler night, watching stars. I came to cherish the pace and lifestyle demanded by the heat. It slowed me down so that I could appreciate and learn from simplicity.

The odor that greeted me when I stepped outside the comfort of the plane made it obvious that we were no longer in the United States. It wasn't a smell that made you gag or was unbearable. In fact, I got used to it very quickly and came to not notice it at all. But it did remind you, as if it was not obvious from the streets of Port-au-Prince that extreme poverty—poverty like nothing I had ever seen—was everywhere.

These two first impressions do not diminish the truth that people are the same everywhere, at least in regard to their dreams, desires, joys, and hope. I learned more about the rest of the world from that first ten-day trip to Haiti, and more about mission outreach, than all my stateside mission trips combined.

We arrived in Haiti just seven months after a devastating earthquake killed over 316,000 people. It injured thousands more and cause an outbreak of several water-borne diseases. The capital city was still filled with tent cities, and the streets were still inundated with massive piles of rubble still waiting to be removed. There were still many desperate souls sticking their emaciated hands through the airport fence, seeking a meager coin or two. I must say that I did not experience culture shock or fear, but I did experience a cornucopia of emotions and a plethora of visual stimulations that were beyond anything I could put words to. The best description of how I felt about my first contact with Haiti, especially as we drove through the streets, is that I experienced an awakening!

I am eternally thankful for my friends Jay and Harriett, who encouraged me to step outside my comfort zones as a Christian. They invited me to be a part of this Haiti adventure, and it changed my life forever! The seeds I would cultivate from these faithful servants were seeds of goodness.

Jay has served as a UMC pastor for well over forty years. He was a past member of the cabinet serving as a district superintendent. His ministry accomplishments and high integrity are inspiring to say the least. His wisdom, along with many gifts and graces, are so very evident in the very successful track record he accumulated at every single pastoral appointment. Lives were changed for the better everywhere he served.

Harriett, his devoted wife, is so much more than a pastor's spouse, as if that would not be enough. Harriett also practiced a tremendous ministry that enveloped her gift of encouragement as well as gifts and graces of wisdom, compassion, and service.

Together, Jay and Harriett are responsible for bringing hundreds of people to Christ. They are a true reflection of devout discipleship and a loving spirit. Their zeal for mission service has inspired many!

If not for Jay and Harriett, I would not have experienced the world outside my little corner of Winchester, VA, and home. If not for their love, wisdom, and guidance, I would not have been able to grow as a human being, a Christian, and as a pastor. I share all this to say that what I value the most about Jay and Harriett is their friendship and their goodness.

Before they moved away to be closer to their children and grandchildren, they were a safe harbor for my wife and me. Their home was always a place of secure rest. It was a sanctuary where we could say what we needed to say to vent, to rant, to share our heartaches and disappointments, and to just be accepted for who God made us to be!

The seeds Jay and Harriett planted in our lives would broaden my world and grow within me an enhanced view and appreciation for the world that exists outside of our safe and comfortable lives. I love Jay and Harriett and appreciate the seeds they planted in me. I believe they have been fruitful.

I went on to lead a mission team back to Haiti in 2014 and again in 2017. Following are two sermons I preached upon arriving back home from my first two Haiti trips. The first was delivered on mission Sunday at Burnt Factory UMC on September 19, 2010. The second sermon was delivered on Mother's Day on May 11, 2014.

I believe these sermons will perhaps give insight and evidence to the fruitfulness of the seeds that were planted by my two most wonderful, faithful friends!

Sermon on Psalm 91:1–6, 14–16,
"We Have Nothing to Fear"

He who dwells in the shelter of the Most High will rest in the shadow of the Almighty. I will say of the LORD, "He is my refuge and my fortress, my God, in whom I trust." Surely, he will save you from the fowler's snare and from the deadly pestilence. He will cover you with his feathers, and under his wings you will find refuge; his faithfulness will be your shield and rampart. You will not fear the terror of night, nor the arrow that flies by day, nor the pestilence that stalks in the darkness, nor the plague that destroys at midday. Psalm 91:1–6

Because he loves me," says the LORD, "I will rescue him; I will protect him, for he acknowledges my name. He will call on me, and I will answer him; I will be with him in trouble, I will deliver him and honor him. With long life I will satisfy him and show him my salvation." Psalm 91:14–16

You know we all some fears in life, don't we? We fear all kinds of things. Fear of heights, fear of enclosed spaces, fear of bugs, fear of flying; the list goes on and on. There were two explorers on a jungle safari when their fears came to life. As they were walking in the bush, a ferocious lion appeared right in front of them. The first explorer said, "Now, don't panic, remember in that book we read that said if this happens, just stand our ground, stay perfectly still, and look the lion right in the eye and he will turn and run away." The second explorer responded, "Well you've read the book and I've read the book, the question is, has the lion read the book?"[1]

And the question for us today is: have we read the book that will relieve our fears?

I guess the most common fear we struggle with is the fear of the dark. A mother asked her six-year-old son to go to the pantry down in the cellar and get her a can of tomato soup. The little boy protested and said, "It was dark down there." The mom said, "Don't worry, Jesus will be with you." Well the little boy made his way to the pantry door and just as he was about to go in, he reached his hand through the door and said, "Jesus, if you're in there, can you hand me a can of tomato soup?"[2]

On our recent mission trip to Haiti, our team stayed with a wonderful family who lived on the outskirts of a small town called Arcahaie. We were away from the hustle and bustle of the Capital city of Port of Prince and were actually living in what we would call, "the country." There was no electricity except for an old generator. Our hosts would, very sparingly, crank it up from time to time, to either provide for worship services in their church or to provide light and some entertainment for us, their guests.

They did this, even though it was an extreme expense for them, and they seemed glad to indulge us. The point I want to make is that when night fall came, it was dark! I mean dark! There was only the light from the brilliant, star-filled, night sky. If there was no moon, it was so dark that you could not see the hand in front of your face. But oh, that night sky, you could see, unfettered by artificial light, every single star, you could pick out planets, you could see the Milky Way, in all its brilliance. We didn't need television or other distractions to whittle away time and entertain us, we could look at the night sky and be comforted by God's glory! And as dark as it was, we knew we need not fear it, for God's presence and promise was so real; so very much felt; so wonderfully made manifest in our lives; that there was no doubt of the Holy Spirit's protection. "The Lord is my light and my salvation" Psalm 27:1

The family we stayed and lived with, ate with, and worshiped with, became for us the face of the Haitian people and fears and doubts that we brought with us were soon vanquished in the light of their compassionate and overwhelming hospitality, love, hope, and faithfulness. We came to minister to them, we came to be the face of Jesus to them, we came to lift them up out of their despair and be a breath of fresh air to an oppressed and hopeless people! We came to bring light and what we found were a people who were resilient, a people who had dignity and faith and hope and trust in God's goodness and providence!

What we discovered were a people who were not living in the dark or were afraid it! What we found were a people, who in their extreme poverty, were richer than most! Why?

Because they knew, they knew, that they lived, not in shacks without electricity, not in shanty's without water and sewer, not in tents without common necessities, no! They knew that they lived in the shelter of the most high God and that they abided in the shadow of the Almighty and they knew that they would, one way or the other, be delivered from the fowlers snare and covered by the feathers of God's love.

You see, they didn't fear the night and they didn't fear the day! In their poverty, in their lack of material processions, they gained an understanding of what real faith is, and by professing that faith, by acknowledging that everything they had, as meager and wanting as it was, was a blessing from God; they understood, perhaps better than anyone, what hope is!

Why were they able to show us this hope? Why were they willing to be a witness to us? Why did they open and take such pride in presenting to us their home. Why did they show us such hospitality? Why, when we came to minister to them, we found that they ministered to us?

It is summed up in the words of our translator and interpreter, a godly man, named Joseph who simply said, "Pastor Steve we know that you love us, by coming here to our country, and we love you, and we know that the grace of God has covered you and us." He said, "Pastor Steve, you are my brother."

Even though Haiti has buried 316,000 people, have many more bodies still trapped under rubble, who perhaps will never be buried or identified. Even though they have been decimated by disease, even though they have been abused by their own government's greed, even though they have been falsely labeled as voodoo practitioners and godless people, even though they have a non-existent economy and have to live with no clean water, electricity, infrastructure, or health care. Even though they have no work and have been victimized and held down by their own government. Even though they have faced all these things, the people of Haiti, by a wide margin, are a people who still trust God and who believe with all their hearts that God will deliver them one day and that God will show them his salvation! They live in the shelter of the most-high God and abide in the shadow of the Almighty and they believe that God is their fortress and refuge! And they do not live in fear! The question is: can we say the same?

It seems to me that one of the biggest problems plaguing us today is that for some strange reason, we; who have so much; who have been blessed beyond imagination; seem to be living in fear. We have the best health care in the world! We have the richest standard of living. We have an infrastructure that surpasses all countries. We can go to the store anytime and eat any food imaginable. We can go to the hospital and be treated, whether we have money or not. We can have an emergency team on the site of an accident within ten minutes or less. We can go to any drinking fountain in the whole country and not worry about contaminated water. We have freedom to say what we want, do what we want, within the framework of a legal system that is also the envy of the world. We can have an attorney represent us whether we can pay or not. We have peaceful exchange of leadership. Every time an election is held, we don't have a military takeover. We have a system of government that rivals any in the history of the world. We have liberty and the right to pursue happiness. We have education that is available to anyone. We have so much and yet we seem to be living in fear. What are we afraid of?

If we are placing our trust in material things and if we are placing our soul security in the hands of the government than shame on us for our security comes from God Almighty and we should be placing our trust, not in what we have accumulated and not in what we have built and not in our military, but in our relationship to Christ Jesus!

The author of 1st Timothy tells us in the sixth chapter: "Command those who are rich in this present world not to be arrogant nor to put their hope in wealth, which is so uncertain, but to place their hope in God, who richly provides us with everything. Command them to do good, to be rich in good deeds, and to be generous and willing to share. In this way they will lay up treasure for themselves as a firm foundation for the coming age, so that they may take hold of the life that is truly life." 1 Timothy 6:17–19

From today's Psalm: "Those who love me, I will deliver; I will protect those who know my name. When they call on me, I will answer them; I will be with them in trouble; I will rescue them and honor them. With long life I will satisfy them and show them my salvation." Psalm 91:14–16

It's alright to be afraid, but we do not need to live in fear; our Lord and our Almighty God is in control! He has not forsaken us and he has not abandoned the people of Haiti. In our riches and fullness, have we become empty and have they, in their poverty and emptiness, become full? St. Paul tells us that we are supposed to "live by faith, not by sight." 2 Corinthians 5:7

John tells us that we are to "walk in the light!" 1 John 1:7

We need not live in fear; we need not let the troubles of the world or the worries of the day steal our light. We don't need to fear the dark, we don't need to fear those things that go bump in the night. We don't need to fear that illness; we don't need to fear that bankruptcy; we don't need to fear getting older; we don't need to fear losing our house; we don't need to fear all those things that are of darkness because; "God is light! And in him there is no darkness! If we claim to have fellowship with him yet walk in the darkness, we lie and do not live by the truth. But if we walk in the light, as he is in the light, we have fellowship with one another, and the blood of Jesus purifies us from all sin!" 1 John 1:6–7

God did not bring calamity upon the people of Haiti, no more than God brought disaster to New Orleans or anywhere else. God does not bring illness and darkness into our lives. God does not will for us to suffer. Listen, we live in a world not as God intended for his children; we live in a fallen state. We live, by our choice, in a condition where bad things happen to good people. God is not absent from our suffering; God is intimately involved. Have we forgotten the extent to which God had gone to show us his love? Have we forgotten that he sacrificed His only son, that he watched has that beloved son went through the mockery and shame of an unjust and merciless trial? Have we forgotten that he watched his son hung up in pain and agony upon a cross of our making? Have we forgotten that "God so loved the world that he gave is only begotten son so that whosoever believeth in him shall not perish, but have everlasting life?" John 3:16

God hasn't turned his back, God is here! God is with us when we suffer. God cries with us, suffers with us, agonizes with us; his tears are mingled with ours. God has not abandoned us and God will not forsake us! We do not need to fear the dark, for God, Emmanuel, the light of the world, is with us!

In times of darkness, when we are walking in the valley of the shadow of death, we can have confidence in God's eternal love. When life comes at us hard and things have been turned upside down, we can have security in our darkness for we know that God loves us. Whatever you may be facing today; know that if you dwell in the shelter of the most high then you will rest in the shadow of the Almighty.

Mother's Day 2014 Psalm 23 (KJV) "The Sights and Sounds of Haiti"

"The LORD *is my shepherd; I shall not want.* He maketh me to lie down in green pastures: he leadeth me beside the still waters. He restoreth my soul: he leadeth me in the paths of righteousness for his name's sake. Yea, though I walk through the valley of the shadow of death, I will fear no evil: for thou art with me; thy rod and thy staff they comfort me. Thou preparest a table before me in the presence of mine enemies: thou anointest my head with oil; my cup runneth over. Surely goodness and mercy shall follow me all the days of my life: and I will dwell in the house of the LORD *forever.*" Psalm 23 (KJV)

I have traveled to Haiti two times in the last four years and both times I have been overwhelmed with an intense and emotional feeling of being somehow swept back into time. Both trips, but especially this one, as our team journeyed to a remote village on a remote island, I felt as if I had been transported back to first century Palestine. I cannot explain it but I also cannot deny it. The sights and sounds along with the people and environment of this tiny village, named Source A Philippe on the island of La Gonave, brought to life in my mind, my heart, and my very soul, what I believe it must have been like when Jesus walked the earth.

As we were waiting to board the old wooden sail boat that would take us across the sea, from the mainland of Haiti to La Gonave, I thought about how Jesus walked along the shore of the sea of Galilee and how he called out to Peter and Andrew and then to James and John. I could almost hear him saying, "Come follow me, I will make you fishers of men." Mark 1:17

As I smelled the sea air and heard the water gently lap upon the shore, I could almost see them dropping their nets, and following Jesus.

On the return voyage, it was early in the morning, and just before the sun started to come up, I could clearly, imagine in my mind's eye, Jesus coming across the water. I could see him as clear as anything and I could hear the words, "Take courage, it is I, don't be afraid." Matthew 14:27

After we arrived at the village, I watched an old man riding his donkey in the dust and dirt and I could hear the old donkey clicking its hooves against the rocks. These words came, without hesitation into my mind, "Hosanna to the Son of David! Blessed is he who comes in the name of the Lord! Hosanna in the highest!" Matthew 21:9 It was as if I was watching Jesus riding into Jerusalem.

We sat down to eat one night and on the table were fish and bread and I thought of the five thousand and I heard these words come into my heart, "Taking the five loaves of bread and two fish and looking up to heaven, he gave thanks and broke the loaves. Then he gave them to the disciples to set before the people. They all ate and were satisfied." Luke 9:16–17

We were satisfied that night too, with food and with fellowship and with humility that we were being fed so graciously and abundantly by those who had so very little. We felt as if Jesus was, indeed, feeding us.

Just the next day, we provided a meal of beans and rice to the children of the village. As they came one by one with smiling faces and empty stomachs, I thought how precious life is. Over several days, we played with the children and did crafts and watched movies with them. Many times, we would have two and three on our laps at a time. The words of Jesus took on new meaning, "Let the little children come to me, and do not hinder them, for the Kingdom of Heaven belongs to such as these." Matthew 19:14 And I came to understand in a new way, how precious innocence is. I watched goats running to and fro. I watched them as they walked the paths and mingled with the people and I thought of the day when the, "Son of man will come in His glory and all the angels with him and all the nations of the world will be gathered before him, and he will separate the people one from the other as a shepherd separates sheep from goats." Matthew 25:31–32

As I listened to the bleats of the young goats yearning for their mothers; I contemplated my own desire to be comforted by my heavenly Father.

There were chickens and roosters running around everywhere and in the middle of the night, just about every night, there was this old rooster that would crow and crow and crow. The agony of Peter's denial of Jesus was made real that night! "Then Peter remembered the word Jesus had spoken: "Before the rooster crows, you will disown me three times. And he went outside and wept bitterly." Matthew 26:75

As I listened to that old rooster crow, I was reminded of my own sin and unworthiness and even more, I was reminded of the great love it took to wash me clean of those sins. Peter came to know it too! That no matter what we have done, God's love and grace are still available.

The whole time I was experiencing the sights and sounds of Haiti and especially as I was experiencing the people, I was struck with how happy the children were and how hopeful the adults were. Every day, I was hearing in my "self-talk" the words of Jesus, "Therefore, I tell you, do not worry about your life, what you will eat or drink; or about your body, or what you will wear. Is not life more important than food and the body more important than clothes? Look at the birds of the air; they do not sow or reap or store away in barns, and yet your heavenly Father feeds them. Are you not more valuable than they? Who of you by worrying can add a single hour to his life?" Matthew 6:25–27 "Seek ye first the Kingdom of God and His righteousness and all these things will be given to you as well." Matthew 6:33

No matter where you are in this world, no matter how rich or poor, the sound of children playing and laughing, the sight of children smiling, the joyous hope of innocence, is a gift from God! These children blessed us so much and taught us so much. These children had nothing! When I say nothing, I mean nothing, and yet they had everything, for they were happy, were content, joyous, and thankful for everything. All they wanted was love!

I was so honored to meet the matriarchs of the village. They were also the sewing guild, a group of woman who were trying to start a business so as to infuse the local economy. They were the collective wisdom of the village and they lived out the last chapter of the book of Proverbs for they were, "Worth far more rubies. Her husband has full confidence in her. She brings him good, not harm, all the days of her life. She selects wool and flax and works with eager hands. She gets up while it is still dark; she provides food for her family; she sets about her work vigorously her arms are strong for the task. She sews that her trading is profitable, and her lamp does not go out at night. She opens her arms to the poor and extends her arms to the needy. She makes linen garments and sells them. She is clothed with strength dignity. She speaks with wisdom. Charm is deceptive and beauty is fleeting; but a woman who fears the Lord is to be praised." Proverbs 31:10–31

These women worked their fingers to the bone keeping their homes, feeding their families, going to Bible studies at night, and supporting their husbands, who were away much of the time, trying to find work. They indeed were to be praised!

Since it is Mother's Day, the closing remembrance from Haiti, from the little village of Source A Philippe on the island of La Gonave is one about a mother. It seems that after dark one evening, this young woman, who was seven months pregnant, was having some problems. She had experienced complications with an earlier pregnancy and she was experiencing some symptoms that alarmed her. The nurses went over her with a fine-tooth comb and found nothing. She just seemed to be overwhelmed, tired, restless, and mostly scared.

The nurses called me and the other pastors in our group to come and pray over her and lay hands upon her. I grabbed her hand as she was laying there in that clinic hospital bed and the others gathered round and we all laid hands upon her and through our interpreter prayed prayers of healing and peace and blessed assurance upon this frightened young woman. It was an experience I will never forget.

Shortly after we left, the nurses told us that she was better and that the only medicine she needed was the assurance that God loved her and that Jesus held her tight in his loving arms. Her vital signs stabilized and she began to find that mysterious peace, that peace that surpasses all understanding!

One of the most amazing parts of this experience was the fact that outside the medical clinic, outside and all around the room where this young mother was lying, there were people from all over the village. There must have been at least thirty villagers who were concerned about this young mother and especially about her unborn child. They were praying and were not going to leave until they knew their friend was going to be alright. She was a good mother, a mother who was trying to take care of and raise all of her children with the love of Jesus. This experience, I believe with all my heart, was the best example of what it means to embrace the living word of God and to trust in Jesus. It was one of the best examples of what I believe it is to understand the holiness of scripture. When the peace of God came upon this young mother; I believe she epitomized the meaning of the Psalm 23, for she knew without a shadow of a doubt that:

"The Lord is her shepherd and that she need not be in want. That her Lord makes her lie down in green pastures and that he leads her beside still waters. That he, the Lord, restores her soul and leads her to the right path! She knew that even though she thought she was walking through the valley of death, that she need not fear any evil, because the Lord was with her. She had nothing to fear for her Lord would prepare a table before her in the very presence of her enemies, in the very presence of those who would steal her peace. She knew, when all is said and done, that her cup overflowed, her head was anointed with healing oil and surely goodness and mercy would follow her forever and that when all is said and done, she would dwell in the house of the Lord forever!" Psalm 23 KJV

This young and scared mother, who lived in utter poverty, who lived in horrendous conditions. This mother, who had no reason for hope other than the hope found through Jesus Christ; understood and lived out the power of the resurrection and the truth of scripture better than just about any person I had seen before.

On this Mother's Day, let us all come to the truth, cling to the truth, hang on to the truth; that Jesus is Lord and holds us all in His powerful and loving nail scarred hands! In the midst of our deepest fears, where does our help come? It comes from the Lord!

Let those who have ears to hear, hear the word of God today and let all who hear the word of God today be doers of that word and embrace the peace of Almighty God. Let us be thankful and let us always understand that the Lord is our shepherd and we need not be in want for God will restore our soul and the Lord will lead us to still waters and green pastures. Amen."

Seeds of goodness sowed through the love of mission as motivated by the love of neighbor are perhaps seeds worth considering!

Thank you, Jay and Harriett, for sowing seeds of goodness and of God's love. Thank you for being a safe harbor in the storm and for your words of encouragement and love.

"Through Jesus, therefore, let us continually offer to God a sacrifice of praise, the fruit of lips that confess his name. And do not forget to do good and to share with others, for with such sacrifices God is pleased" (Hebrews 13:15–16).

"Do all the good you can, By all the means you can, In all the ways you can, In all the places you can, At all the times you can, To all the people you can, As long as ever you can."[3]

"Don't judge each day by the harvest you reap but by the seeds you plant."[4]

Chapter 7

Seeds of Peace
Elmer and Grace, "And They
Say There's No God"

There is nothing that can quite compare to the heavenly smell and extravagant taste of fried bread! If you have never tasted fried bread done right—southern style—you have not lived a full life! Grace was who I referred to as an old-fashioned, southern, lard-slinging, grease-guzzling, country cook!

It was all about taste, my friends, and only Grace could place her homemade bread dough in her hundred-year-old cast-iron skillet and create heaven on earth! That bread would come off that skillet with an aroma that brought instant comfort, mixed with anticipation, unequalled by even Christmas morning standards! That bread would be hot, which made it so very easy for the homemade butter to run all over it like ice cream over the face of a four-year-old on a hot summer day! And if you decided to place apple butter or strawberry preserves upon that hot bread, it would conjure up feelings of satisfaction that are nothing short of what it must be like in heaven!

Grace was the better half of the great duo known as Elmer and Grace. My wife Melanie and I were both nineteen when we met Elmer and Grace. They were in their midfifties and they were unlike any older people my nineteen years of life had ever experienced. They were fun and they were genuinely interested in our lives.

Elmer and Grace lived in a very humble home at the base of the Great North Mountain on about 150 acres. They were surrounded on all sides by Elmer's brothers and sisters that also inherited land from their parents. Their little home was nestled right up to where the pasture land met the forest, and their front yard was filled with poplar trees that looked like they actually touched the sky. Deer were so plentiful, you had to dodge them on the way up their driveway.

The name of their quaint abode was Birdsong because they had a great love for birdwatching. They even had a pet parakeet that they would allow to fly around the house for the first five minutes of our visits. My wife Melanie a person who does not appreciate birds, will never forget when Petie landed on her head! They were the most extraordinary couple and the most content people I think I ever knew. Their home was truly a place of beauty and peace. Their home was very small but very comfortable. Their heat was furnished by a wood stove, and the entire back half of their abode served as a storage/workshop area.

We met Elmer and Grace through a mutual friend who was a rock climbing buddy of mine. We had a group of five devotees who participated in this sport. We also loved backpacking and hiking and camping. We spent many joyous weekends enjoying, along with our significant others, the wonders and majesty of the great outdoors.

Rock climbing in the seventies was a fairly new sport that relatively few people participated in. As our love for the sport grew, we decided, as East Coast inhabitants, to plan an extended trip out west where the big mountains were. This is where Elmer and Grace came into the picture. My friend knew that they had traveled extensively in the Rocky Mountains and camped the entire trip. He also knew that they had a love for the outdoors and for young people. He also knew that they had personal knowledge and experience regarding many of the locations we were looking to visit. They even had old-fashioned slides of their journeys. For anyone forty-five and under, slides were picture negatives that were shown on a wall or a screen by a specialized projector. I must admit that I miss good old-fashioned slideshows. They sure were a lot more fun than perusing through an iPhone.

In any event, this common appreciation and love for God's creation, for the west, for camping, for life, and for people, brought us all together, and none of us would ever be the same.

Elmer and Grace were old-school Assembly of God folks. They never tried to beat us heathens over the head with the Bible, and they never—not once—lectured us or judged us. They simply lived their faith with confidence and zeal. They loved us all and provided many hours of slideshows, meals, and mentoring! They prayed before meals, they prayed for us every day, they taught Sunday school for most of their lives, they supported a missionary to India, and they made everyone feel special. They had the gift of hospitality and intercessory prayer. They also, no matter what life brought them, bestowed a peace that surpassed our human understanding. They truly and genuinely embraced the peace of God. They shattered any stupid stereotypes I had conjured up in my mind about their faith practices.

On one trip out west together, we came to a scenic overlook that provided my first glimpses of the Grand Tetons mountain range. I just stood there with my mouth hanging open, dumbfounded by the magnificence of God's creation. I was in awe of the magnitude and scope and grandeur of what I was seeing. Elmer, in his usual humble demeanor, looked at me and just quietly said, "And they say there is no God."

His simple and honest comment helped to strengthen my resolve to advance my discipleship and to see the beauty of God in His creation. I decided I would never take for granted the beautiful world God provided for us. I also found that I truly cherished what Elmer and Grace had. They loved each other dearly and lived to make each other happy. They sacrificed for each other. They loved life and participated in life in ways that, to this day, have me tired just thinking about their many adventures. I could share an entire book on their exploits, adventures, interests, and stories.

Years later—after marriages, children, divorces, and life getting in the way—many of our original group of thrill seekers, which

Elmer named the West Gang, started to go their own ways. The group dissolved, and it was never quite the same. I kept my relationship with Elmer and Grace; and as they grew older and became less active, I continued to visit them, though not as frequently. When Elmer developed brain cancer, I was privileged to be a part of a team of friends and family that took him to his radiation treatments.

I arrived at Birdsong on that brisk March morning just minutes after he passed, and just like he lived, he died in complete and total peace. Grace would follow the love of her life several years later, succumbing to kidney failure, and I must tell you, it was my honor to officiate at their humble graveside services.

Elmer and Grace loved God with every fiber of their being, and they loved their neighbor as themselves. I believed they lived and embraced what Paul shared in Philippians 4:11–13 when he said, "For I have learned to be content whatever the circumstances. I know what it is to be in need and I know what it is to have plenty. I have learned the secret of being content in any and every situation, whether well fed or hungry, whether living in plenty or want. I can do everything through him who gives me strength."

Elmer and Grace made people feel special. They embraced life and had a joy and humor about them that radiated a warmth that only the Holy Spirit could provide. They had the kind of joy that could only be from total, uncompromising faith in Jesus Christ. They had the kind of joy and confident wisdom in their witness that can only be realized from absolute perfect peace.

I miss my friends and that special season in our young lives when these two "old people" took us under their wings and taught us what marriage is supposed to look like, what discipleship is supposed to look like, and what the peace of God is supposed to look like!

Paying attention to young people and making them feel special are seeds worth considering. The seeds they planted in me were of great variety, and I have cherished nurturing those seeds for the glory of God. I must admit that I struggle mightily with finding consistent peace, but because of Elmer and Grace, I plan to keep trying.

"Make every effort to live in peace with everyone and to be holy; without holiness no one will see the Lord" (Hebrews 12:14).

"Peace begins with a smile."[1]

Lord, make me an instrument of your peace. Where there is hatred, let me bring love. Where there is offence, let me bring pardon. Where there is discord, let me bring union. Where there is error, let me bring truth. Where there is doubt, let me bring faith. Where there is despair, let me bring hope. Where there is darkness, let me bring your light. Where there is sadness, let me bring joy. O Master, let me not seek as much to be consoled as to console, to be understood as to understand, to be loved as to love, for it is in giving that one receives, it is in self-forgetting that one finds, it is in pardoning that one is pardoned, it is in dying that one is raised to eternal life.[2]

Chapter 8

Seeds of Gentleness
Jonah, the Greatest Listener

The *Baker Evangelical Dictionary of Biblical Theology* describes the spiritual gift of mercy as "sensitivity of disposition and kindness of behavior founded on strength and prompted by love."[1] I would add that those who exude gentleness are very good listeners and encouragers!

Have you ever had a friend that could just listen? I mean be there for you through thick and thin and never yield to the temptation to give advice? Have you ever had a friend that would listen to your problems without complaining? Have you ever had a friend that you could yell at and they would understand, the kind of friend that you could always trust? I was lucky to have that kind of friend. His name was Jonah.

I knew Jonah for nine years, and in all that time, he never spoke an unkind word about anybody. He never judged people. I don't think he had a mean bone in his body. My gentle friend could be compulsive sometimes. He liked to have order in his life. I would tease him and suggest that it maybe this trait came from his German heritage. Jonah tended to want his life regimented, and sometimes, he could be a little demanding. But these were, at best, minor personality traits that didn't affect our friendship at all.

Jonah would listen to me for hours and was especially attentive when I was trying to figure out whether God had called me to pastoral ministry. I would ramble on for hours, writing down the pros and the cons. He would quietly, and without annoyance, continue to listen to me try and ascertain whether God would sincerely call the likes of me. As I went back and forth over this decision for five years, he just reassuringly would give me a look or put out his hand to mine and let me know everything was going to be all right. He would even give me a kiss on the cheek now and then to let me know he loved me.

If you haven't had a friend like that, I'm sorry. Everyone needs a friend like Jonah.

Jonah and I loved God's creation and the great outdoors, and we would take long walks together discussing all kinds of things. And the longer we would walk, the more I would talk and the more he would listen. I loved that old guy, and I believe he loved me. No one could listen the way he could and not love you.

He was the gentlest soul I had ever known. Jonah started to have some health concerns, and I was very concerned and upset when he was diagnosed with pancreatic cancer. It was my turn to be his friend. I helped him the best I could, and as I watched him slowly get sicker and sicker, I understood just how much this good friend meant to me.

I nursed him and loved him, but the inevitable was creeping into my mind. How much longer was I going to have my good friend, my confidant, my gentle listener? The doctors said he had about a year, but it ended up being well over two years before he passed. It was a great privilege to be with him and to hold him when he closed his eyes for the last time.

My friend taught me so much about patience and unconditional love, but most of all, he planted seeds of gentleness in my soul. He showed me what it was like to be a true friend. He loved me without reservation and helped me to make the most important decision I ever made. I will never forget this friend of mind, this friend that provided the best gift a friend could ever offer—the gift of gentle listening!

As I reflect on his life and all that Jonah meant to me. When I reflect on his death and resurrection, I am reminded and God has assured me that yes indeed all dogs do go to heaven! The seeds planted in me from my loyal and beloved German shorthaired pointer, Jonah, will stay with me forever! He was the most gentle and patient listener that I ever encountered! His love was truly unconditional! The unconditional love of our pets along with their loyal devotion bring us great joy. Their gentle lives provide seeds that are worthy of consideration.

"The wolf will live with the lamb, the leopard will lie down with the goat, the calf and the lion and the yearling together; and a little child will lead them. The cow will feed with the bear, their young will lie down together, and the lion will eat straw like the ox" (Isaiah 11:6–7).

"God will prepare everything for our perfect happiness in heaven, and if it takes my dog being there, I believe he'll be there."[2]

PART 2

Holy Spirit Seeds

We have different gifts, according to the grace given to each of us. If your gift is prophesying, then prophesy in accordance with your faith; if it is serving, then serve; if it is teaching, then teach; if it is to encourage, then give encouragement; if it is giving, then give generously; if it is to lead do it diligently; if it is to show mercy, do it cheerfully.

—Romans 12:6–8

Your spiritual gifts were not given for your own benefit but for the benefit of others, just as other people were given gifts for your benefit.[1]

—Rick Warren

Chapter 9

Seeds of Mercy
Edna and Georgie, Beloved
Mother and Grandmother

Edna

As long as I can remember, my mother, who was named Edna after her maternal grandmother, has practiced the spiritual gift of mercy. This gift is manifested in compassionate care of the vulnerable. Nurses, for example, usually exhibit this gift. My maternal great-grandmother had this gift (see chapter 1); and her daughter, my grandmother, as you will read in this chapter, also possessed this gift. My mother, by the power of the Holy Spirit, has been the recipient of these generational legacy seeds that have continued to harvest great fruit.

One of the great qualities inherent in this gift of mercy is that the care of others never seems to be a burden. Tending to the needs of others, for people who possess this gift, is not based upon guilt, duty, expectation, or some sort of spiritual barter. Rather, it is practiced with a profound sense of joy. No better example of this is my mother's sacrificial and devotional care of her father and her brother-in-law as they were coming to the end of their lives. First, let's explore her care of her father as he was nearing his last days.

Years after my grandmother had died, my grandfather grew old and reached a point when he became very sick. He had been an exceptionally healthy person for most of his life. Some would say, he was too ornery to get sick. In any event, my mother was tasked with bringing him to live out his final days with her. What made this so poignant and deserving of respect was that my mother took care of a man that never once expressed love or pride in the very daughter tasked with his care.

Without wishing to malign my grandfather's memory, suffice it to say he was not the warmest or most compassionate person to walk this old earth. Maybe, he was a product of his upbringing. Perhaps having to provide for his family during the Depression was too stressful. Perhaps the death of a four-year-old daughter from diphtheria played a part in his personality. I don't know what made him oblivious to the vital nurturing demands of a parent; but they were missing, at least, toward my mother.

He had some endearing qualities, and he did provide during a difficult time in our country's history. But for whatever reason, I think it fair to say that he was unable to exhibit a nurturing, grace-filled disposition. My maternal grandfather worked hard, provided food and a house—those necessary things for survival. He did, what I believe to be, the best he was capable of. Unfortunately, he was void of any true altruism. Now, let me say that this was my mother's experience.

My mother wished that just one time, just once, that her father would have uttered the words, "Thank you my beautiful daughter. I love you, and I am proud of you!" It would not happen. My mother did the sacrificial and quite strenuous work of caring for a father from whom she never felt loved. She did the hard stuff; and it was only when the gangrene traveling up is legs became too severe for her to treat that he was placed in a care facility where, at ninety-two just a few days later, he took his final breaths on this old earth.

That same year, my mother was also called upon to provide aid for her brother-in-law when he became homebound from the effects of lung cancer. His wife possessed many gifts, but the gift of mercy was not one of them. So once again, my mother took into her home a person who needed care, compassion, and a safe place to die. My mother would say many times, what a wonderful privilege it was to care for Smitty. That was her nickname for him. They had many tender moments, and his gratitude and humility was extraordinary. My uncle, it could be said, suffered well and kept the faith to the very end.

My mother planted seeds in me from using her gifts and modeling what Christian mercy truly looked like. My uncle planted seeds in me for showing me how a Christian dies. His faith never faltered and his gratitude never waned, even while navigating the terrible assault of lung cancer.

My mother's obedience to the Lord on using her gifts for the kingdom helped allow my uncle to die with dignity. My uncle and my grandfather were two very different men; but my mother, using the seeds planted in her from her mother and grandmother, provided grace, forgiveness, compassion, and sacrificial care. She did this as empowered, equipped, and enabled by the Holy Spirit. She did this not for accolades or blessings but because she saw the face of Christ in them. And the true fruit from these seeds of mercy was that they saw in their dying days the face of Christ in my mother.

Is it any wonder that my sister became a nurse and her daughter became a nurse? Is it any wonder that my brother became a doctor and that I eventually became a pastor?

Perhaps, legacy seeds are seeds worth considering!

"Praise be to the God and Father of our Lord Jesus Christ, the Father of compassion and the God of all comfort, who comforts us in all our troubles, so that we can comfort those in any trouble with the comfort we ourselves receive from God" (2 Corinthians 1: 3–4).

"You gain strength, courage, and confidence by every experience in which you really stop to look fear in the face. You must do the things which you think you cannot do."[1]

"Honor your father and your mother, so that you may live long in the land the Lord your God is giving you" (Exodus 20:12).

Georgie

The Coffelt family, if not the poorest family in the county, would be considered in the top five. If not for the church and the community, they would have not survived the Great Depression. My maternal grandmother, Georgie, would always find ways to help this family. These altruistic endeavors were always more challenging in that she did not have the support of her husband. So she would hide the number of eggs gathered each morning so she could take the extra ones to the Coffelt's after her husband would go to work. She did the same, like hiding extra cloth that she would use to sew undergarments for the Coffelt children. She did the same when she would give all the children baths. She found ways to use her God-given gift of mercy because she saw, as her mother before her modeled so beautifully, the face of Jesus in those she ministered too.

Georgie was also tasked with taking care of her bedridden mother-in-law while attending to her own newborn baby. She cared for her, tending to her every need. This was accomplished in an era where there was no indoor plumbing and no heating and air-conditioning. This was a time when you carried water from a spring to the house, and you emptied slop basins every morning. This was an era where everything you did required extra and strenuous work! These examples of joy-filled Christian service and charity would be the catalyst for my mother's sense of service for the kingdom.

Georgie did many other acts of Christian service over her lifetime, a life that unfortunately was cut short by cancer. She was an inspiration to her family and a person who found a way to use her God-given gifts. She loved her family and her Lord.

From my great-grandmother to my grandmother, to my mother, to my sister, seeds of mercy have been scattered, and many have taken root and many have and continue to be fruitful!

One of the greatest gifts we can offer is the joyful sacrificial care of others at their most vulnerable time.

It is seed worth considering!

"Your greatest contribution to the kingdom of God might not be something you do, but someone you raise."[2]

> "Then the King will say to those on his right, 'Come, you who are blessed by my Father; take your inheritance, the kingdom prepared for you since the creation of the world. For I was hungry and you gave me something to eat, I was thirsty and you gave me something to drink, I was a stranger and you invited me in, I needed clothes and you clothed me, I was sick and you looked after me, I was in prison and you came to visit me.'
>
> "Then the righteous will answer him, 'Lord, when did we see you hungry and feed you, or thirsty and give you something to drink? When did we see you a stranger and invite you in, or needing clothes and clothe you? When did we see you sick or in prison and go to visit you?' "The King will reply, 'Truly I tell you, whatever you did for one of the least of these brothers and sisters of mine, you did for me." (Matthew 25:34–40)

"My mother was the most beautiful woman I ever saw. All I am I owe to my mother. I attribute all my success in life to the moral, intellectual and physical education I received from her."[3]

Chapter 10

Seeds of Teachers
Lucille, Twins, and the Two Ediths

Lucille

I have been blessed with wonderful teachers over the years that have planted enduring positive seeds in the developing soil of my soul. I have also been challenged with teachers that have sowed negative seeds that, in hindsight, have also taught me by contrast.

My first junior high Sunday school teacher was a woman named Lucille. Now, I grew up in a very small former EUB rural faith community where everyone knew everyone and where most of the congregation was related, so I knew Lucille was my mother's first cousin. We would visit in each other's homes. Yes, that actually happened. People did visit each other in person! I am positive Lucille taught me many biblical truths and stories; but what I remember most was her great sense of humor, her attitude of joy, and her contagious laugh. She made Sunday school fun, and she never took herself too seriously.

She told this story when visiting in our home one Saturday evening right before Christmas. I was ten years old, and I don't think she thought I could hear the conversation or perhaps that I was not paying attention to the adults. In any event, she said she found herself in a major department store (this would have been in the late sixties) and suffering from a very painful attack of gas. She needed to, how should I delicately say this—expend the abundant buildup of hazardous and pernicious bloat! She had to pass the gas! So, not being able to find the restroom in this huge store and finding expediency to be of the utmost importance, she decided to find an inconspicuous area in the store to achieve her goal.

She spotted a Santa Clause mannequin over in the back corner of the toy section and made her way to the lifeless dummy. With much relief, she preceded with the foul deed, only to realize after she regained her wits that the Santa Clause was not a mannequin after all but the very much alive store Santa taking a break! As she told this embarrassing story on herself, she just laughed and laughed. She said Santa didn't think it was very funny.

Lucille taught me how to laugh at life and laugh at ourselves. She planted seeds in me of humor and laughter!

These are seeds we need today more than ever and certainly seeds worth considering!

"A cheerful heart is good medicine" (Proverbs 17:22).

"A glad heart makes a happy face" (Proverbs 15:13).

The Twins, Mary and Martha

Mary and Martha were fraternal twins who taught fourth grade. I was lucky to have both of them as my teachers. I was also blessed to have them in later years as loyal customers of my HVAC business. They were old-school teachers who remembered each and every student they ever taught. It was remarkable. They obtained a disciplined classroom without being mean. They achieved this with a wonderful balance of accountability, responsibility, and love. Their students knew they were loved.

I was fascinated that neither had ever married and especially enthralled that, even until they died, they continued to dress alike, right down to their jewelry! They referred to each other not by their names but as *sister*.

Each year, I would come to their house to make sure their HVAC equipment was tuned up and functioning at full capacity. I could never leave until I had something to drink and a few cookies. They always inquired about the welfare of my family.

They were inspirational in their approach to life, which was predicated upon their trust in God and commitment to their vocation. They loved children and loved teaching. It was their purpose in life! Mary and Martha lived up to their biblical counterparts in that Martha was outgoing and an organizer, whereas Mary was more genteel and introspective. Even though they had not married and had no children of their own, they ended up with hundreds of children who, like me, has never forgotten them.

They were kind but understood and practiced appropriate discipline. Their classroom and their home was spotless. You could eat off the floor in both places! They were great teachers but humble in spirit. They loved the Lord, and they loved the choices they made in life. They were very content people who enjoyed each other's company. They lived their lives on their terms and enjoyed every minute of it. They sowed seeds of love for all their students, and seeds of contentment and serenity to all those who knew them.

Contentment is such an elusive commodity in today's hurried, competitive world. I don't think we will see the likes of Mary and Martha again; but for me, they were fascinating, unique, and a huge part of my upbringing in small town, America.

I am thankful for many teachers that made a difference in my growth, but I am especially thankful for teachers who were genuine and passionate for their calling. It is the same qualities people respond to in a pastor. Seeds of contentment grown from confidence and love are worth considering!

"I have learned the secret of being content in any and every situation, whether well-fed or hungry, whether living in plenty or want. I can do everything through him who gives me strength" (Philippians 4:12–13).

The Two Ediths

Sometimes, seeds serve as sacrificial training kernels. They are like starter grass seed whose purpose is to grow quickly, to stabilize the ground, and then die off as the permanent seed takes root. Sometimes, this seed can help us understand the value of choice.

In 1969 or '70, I was in the sixth grade and had two teachers by the name of Edith. One was a reading teacher and the other a math teacher. Reading-teacher Edith hated children and made it her goal to see how many kids she could make cry. Even as an eleven-year-old kid, I wondered why she was a teacher. I was committed to not placing myself in her sights, as I witnessed the effectiveness of her attacks on stronger kids than me. So I kept my mouth shut and tried to fly under the radar. I was determined to make it through that year without shedding a tear in front of my classmates. I did achieve my goal, and I also developed compassion for those kids that were not as lucky.

Maybe that was the purpose of those temporary seeds? Nah! She was just plain mean, and in today's world, I doubt she would have been able to retain tenure.

The second Edith taught math, and I got along with her pretty well until she took it upon herself to trade her math degree for a speech therapy degree. You see, I had a speech impediment throughout my elementary and middle-school years.

My particular impediment prevented me from pronouncing *R*'s, and it was especially difficult to pronounce words that had *R* and *L* together. To read aloud in class was torture.

Math teacher Edith knew this but called on me to stand up in class one day and read a math word problem. Now, I had already learned how to deal with the laughter when kids heard me try and pronounce these challenging words. It did not bother me. I learned to use humor to deflect their cruelty. I also had become somewhat of an athlete, and this also helped quell the reactions to my impediment.

In any event, math teacher Edith tried to correct my pronunciation challenges, challenges that speech therapy professionals could not seem to help all in one class. She also chose to provide this insensitive correction in front of the other students. The word problem I was tasked with reading was packed with *R*'s and *L*'s. Oh boy! She made me stand there, with everyone laughing, forcing me to say these words over and over again. "You can say these words correctly, just concentrate! It's just lazy. Come on say it. Say it!"

This is etched in my memory; but thankfully, because of the confidence instilled in me by my parents and because I had some great friends, this potentially devastating, self-esteem–lowering experience did not have the impact on my development that it could have had. I survived sixth grade and considered it a badge of honor to not be broken by either of the two Ediths!

When I got to high school, the impediment just stopped. I don't know if I grew out of it or if God intervened, but it was gone. To tell you the truth, I felt sorry for math teacher Edith, but not too sorry. You see, later in life, like Mary and Martha, math teacher Edith became a loyal customer of my HVAC business. You can't make this irony up!

So this is confession time. I treated her with the utmost respect. I came in the middle of the night when she had a heating problem. I did the furnace maintenance every summer. I was the diligent contractor, but I also tacked on an extra fifteen dollars on each and every service call. I'm sorry, Lord!

Sometimes, we need to sort out the positive seeds from the negative. Jesus taught in another parable that weeds needed to grow along with the wheat. They both had a part to play in our life's journey. Sometimes, we can learn much from the negative seeds that have been cast our way, for they can influence our choices and challenge us to make decisions on how we want to act and what kind of persons we desire to be.

I learned from the two Ediths the kind of person I didn't wish to become. I also learned later in life that I needed to pour out grace upon these ladies as I did not have knowledge of their life journey. Let's face it; we all have challenges that help mold us and make us.

These challenges need not define us, but they can serve to give perspective. My experience with these teachers is very mild compared to the struggles of many underprivileged and poverty-stricken children. My struggles were tame compared to those growing up in abusive and dysfunctional homes. I understand how extremely fortunate I was to be born into my family.

Seeds come to us through many different people and at various times and in contrasting seasons. Perhaps, these seeds are worth considering. We need to keep our eyes and ears open and our soil cultivated, but there will be times when we need to throw away some of those seeds.

"When educating the mind of youth, we must not forget to educate their hearts."[1]

"Not many of you should become teachers, my fellow believers, because you know that we who teach will be judged more strictly" (James 3:1).

"Bear with each other and forgive whatever grievances you may have against one another. Forgive as the Lord forgave you" (Colossians 3:13).

Chapter 11

Seeds of Encouragement
Pastor Bob, "You are that Leader!"

Progressive bulbar palsy is a motor nerve disease which involves the lower motor neurons. These are the neurons that conduct messages from the brainstem and spinal cord to the brain. Symptoms of this cruel disease include but are not limited to: the inability to swallow, weakness in jaw and facial muscles, atrophy of tongue muscle, weakness in limbs, and progressive loss of speech. Some people develop ALS, commonly known as Lou Gehrig's disease, with this condition.

What makes this disease so very sad and insidious is that its victims will retain all their cognitive functions. They will be acutely aware, over an average six-year life expectancy, of every minute decline. While maintaining one's cognitive capabilities could certainly be considered a positive nonsymptom, one cannot help but feel the bittersweetness of this reality.

The symptom in Pastor Bob's case that was so grievous was his loss of speech. The term *ironic* does not quite cover the depth of understanding or despair encountered when a great preacher with immense oratorical skill, with so much more to say, with a gift from the Holy Spirit for sharing the word of God, was struck silent. Pastor Bob was a preacher of high intellect and great skill. He brought many hundreds to the saving grace of our Lord Jesus Christ. He had successful pastorates everywhere he served. Love exuded from this humble man of God. For this disease to steal his voice seems unimaginably severe and unfair.

Pastor Bob came into my life and my church several years before his death, and in that time, we became close friends. At first, he was able to attend church, but that would be short-lived as his disease would soon prevent him from walking. To help Bob communicate, he would use a device where he could type out what he wanted to say and then it would speak for him. It worked well, but Bob did most of his communication with his eyes. The Bible says, "The eye is the lamp of the body. If your eyes are good, your whole body will be full of light" (Matthew 6:22).

Trust me when I say that Bob had good eyes! As we would visit, Bob's eyes would reveal his emotions and his thoughts. They would speak volumes and encompass such feelings as concern, despair, and sadness. His eyes would also shine with joy, faith, humor, hope, and love! I felt more love come from this dear man through his eyes than from anything he could say. Yes, he spoke through tears quite abundantly; but they were tears of pride and love for his family, especially his wife Sandra, his children, and grandchildren.

Bob's soul was intact, and his eyes were good! I never saw regret in those eyes, and I never saw fear either. I never saw anger in those eyes or blame. Bob loved the Lord and perhaps his greatest witness of all was the way he endured and persevered through his illness, all the time trusting in Jesus Christ, His Lord! If I could be just half the pastor that Bob was and if I can accept my destiny half as well as Bob, I would consider it an accomplishment of great magnitude!

Bob had many talents, gifts, graces, and skills, and the one I want to share with you is his love for working with stained glass. He was quite an artist and enjoyed immensely giving his creations away. I have several of his works of art and especially cherish the Christmas star he made for me and another one he made for the church. They will always remind me of the light that came forth not just from his eyes but from his spirit!

Stained glass never shines as bright as it should without light. It is fitting that Bob worked in this medium as he was a beacon of light.

"Let you light shine before men, that they may see your good deeds and praise your Father in heaven" (Matthew 5:16).

Bob, even in the midst of horrendous illness, was still transmitting the glorious light of Christ. Our visits meant the world to me as he would always impart some wonderful nugget of truth or would offer a measure of encouragement. He always inquired about the church and was eager to hear what was happening. He was also always prepared to offer me a word of encouragement and praise. His words to me were kind and genuine, and the letter he wrote me shortly after his voice deserted him means everything to me.

Whenever I get down or depressed, especially in regard to the pandemic and the future of our church and denomination, I get that letter out and read it again. It never fails to lift me up, and as I read it, I can see those wonderful eyes speaking words of love to me all over again.

I will not share the entire letter because it would be gratuitous, but for the sake of this book's subject matter, I will share one section. Bob wrote, "Your spiritual gifts and love have nurtured the growing of BFUMC. I would sense that you would attribute the vitality of the church to other committed lay leaders and not to you alone, but it takes a committed leader to sow that seed and lead the way and you are that leader!"

Bob sowed many seeds of encouragement over his lifetime of ministry, and I was very blessed and privileged to be his pastor and friend during the concluding season of his earthly life. He always wanted to know how the church was doing and how I was doing. Even with the grip of horrendous illness, he was encouraging others. He was still sowing seeds. He was still a pastor. He was still a preacher. I loved Bob and will miss our visits. These are seeds of the highest quality! These are seeds worth considering!

"Each of us may be sure that if God sends us on stony paths, he will provide us with strong shoes."[1]

"Through many dangers, toils and snares, I have already come; tis grace hath brought me safe thus far and grace will lead me home."[2]

"So do not throw away your confidence; it will be richly rewarded. You need to persevere so that when you have done the will of God, you will receive what he has promised" (Hebrews 10:35).

"Have I not commanded you? Be strong and courageous. Do not be afraid; do not be discouraged, for the Lord your God will be with you wherever you go" (Joshua 1:9).

Chapter 12

Seeds of Perseverance
Susan and Barney, Pushing the Rock

Susan and Barney, after dating through college, decided to go their separate ways. They broke up, went on to fall in love with other people, marry, have children, enjoy successful careers, enjoy the fruit of their labor, and basically, live the American dream. Barney was a successful salesman, and Susan, a successful educator. Their children were accomplished, well-adjusted, contributing members of society. For twenty-five years, their lives could not have been better.

It was then that the storms that so frequently show up without warning descended upon these two families. Barney's wife and Susan's husband were stricken with cancer. Barney's and Susan's lives took on the unexpected role of caregivers. For five years, they provided for their beloved partners and aided them in mounting an all-out war against these deadly adversaries.

Barney and Susan fulfilled their marriage vows in every possible scenario, but none more tenaciously than the one that asked, "Will you love each other in sickness and health?" They did everything they could possibly do to make their spouse's last days comfortable and filled with love.

Barney and Susan fulfilled the vow that agreed to being devoted to each other until separated by death.

Susan and Barney lost their spouses about the same time. They were in mourning and in grief about the same time. Both of their lives had been torn asunder, but these devout Christians were healing and becoming new again. After all, they worship the God of resurrection power—the God that brings new life, new opportunities, new growth, and new relationships!

They worship the God "that in all things, works for the good of those who love him, who have been called according to his purpose" (Romans 8:28).

Through a series of God-orchestrated, serendipitous happenings, Barney and Susan rediscovered each other. They had not seen nor spoken to each other since they left college, but our God has a way of making all things new! One thing led to another, and before long, they found themselves dating and falling back in love.

Now, I attended the same church as Susan and played on the softball team with her husband. After I became a pastor and was appointed to another church, I lost contact with Susan and her husband. I knew that her husband had died, but I had not seen them nor spoken to them for years.

Out of the clear blue sky, as Forrest Gump would say, I got a call from Susan. It was so good to hear her voice. She was as giddy as a junior high school girl going to her first dance. She told me the story of her and Barney, and I was so happy for them. She said they were getting married and wanted me to perform the ceremony. They wanted a small wedding and chose to celebrate it at a friend's farm. I was so honored, and I was truly happy for them. Our God is a good and loving God! What a great story, but it is only the beginning.

It was a beautiful autumn day in September when these two wonderful Christians once again entered into the marriage covenant. It was one of the most emotional weddings I ever had the privilege to officiate. Even Barney's former mother-in-law attended to wish the happy couple every blessing. Tears were flowing as the family and guests knew what they had endured and persevered through in their previous marriages. They also knew how strong these two were when it came to doing the hard part of marriage, and nothing is harder than watching the love of your life slowly and methodically waste away from cancer.

It was as if all the emotions of past weddings and past seasons of life were bundled together with the promises of a future season, where love was rekindled and where broken lives were mended. God had brought these two together. Of that, there was no doubt. Resurrection had taken place!

The Bible tells us that "the race is not to the swift or the battle to the strong, nor does food come to the wise or wealth to the brilliant or favor to the learned; but time and chance happen to them all. As fish are caught in a cruel net, or birds are taken in a snare, so men are trapped by evil times that fall unexpectantly upon them" (Ecclesiastes 9:11–12).

Two months after their marriage, Susan suffered a devastating accident. Susan was very athletic, and as she was riding her bike down a steep hill, she struck a car broadside. She broke her neck and would become a quadriplegic. Barney would once again take on the role of caregiver. Susan responded to her accident with the blessed assurance of God's providential care, and Barney responded with complete devotion. They surrendered their plight in life to God's tender mercy.

The best way for me to share the bountiful harvest produced by the many seeds Susan and Barney planted is to share my tribute at her service of death and resurrection.

Service of death and resurrection for Susan May 25, 2019

Years ago, I shared in a sermon, a teaching parable, that little did I know, would become Susan's mantra. Let me share the parable. It's been around for a long time.

"A woman was awakened one night by a great and warm light. Jesus was the light and he told the woman he had work for her to do. He took the woman outside and showed her a huge rock; it must have been 6 feet in circumference. The Lord explained to the woman that he wanted her to push against that rock with all her might. The woman did this day after day; for many years she pushed against the rock. In the scorching heat she pushed, in the cool of spring she pushed. In the bitter cold of winter, she pushed; when she was sick, she pushed, when she was in pain, she pushed. She pushed with all her might against this unyielding rock.

Each night, the woman would return to her home discouraged, she would be sore and worn out; she began to feel her time was being spent in vain. The evil one would start to whisper things in her ear; things like, "you're a failure, why keep trying to move the rock. You will never do it! You're not good enough! You're not strong enough! Why not just go at it half-hearted, just put your time in, just lean against the rock instead of pushing it."

Finally, the woman decided to go to the Lord in prayer. She said, Lord, I have labored long and hard in your service, putting all my strength to do that which you have asked. Yet after all this time, I have not moved the rock at all. What is wrong? Why have I failed?

The Lord, full of compassion, said, 'Beloved, when I asked you to serve me and you accepted, I told you that your task was to push against the rock with all your strength, which you have done. Never once did I mention to you that I expected you to move it. Your task was to push. And now you come to me thinking that you have failed. Look at yourself. Your arms are strong; your back is full of strength and muscles; your hands are calloused; but your grip is sure; your legs are massive and able to stand strong. Through opposition and hard work, you have grown strong. You have been obedient, you have been faithful, and you have trusted me. You have not failed for I never told you to move the rock; I told you to push the rock. And now, my faithful friend, I will move the rock!"[1]

The first time I met with Susan after her accident, she made it clear to me that it was her intention to walk again, to move again, to dance again, to play tennis again, to ride her bike again, to teach again and to garden again. She knew she had to start pushing against the rock and she was going to push every day. She knew there would be hard days and long days when the pushing would take its toll. Susan had down days to be sure, Susan had days of difficulty, days we cannot even, in our wildest dreams, comprehend, but she kept pushing the rock!

Through pushing that rock, Susan touched so many lives and was such an inspiration to so many. Long before her accident, she was making a profound difference in this world. After her accident, her faith, perseverance, endurance, and positive attitude was the epitome of Christian hope! Paul said, in Romans 5 that "We should rejoice in our suffering and that suffering produces perseverance and that perseverance produces character and that character produces hope and that hope (in Christ) would never disappoint." Romans 5:3–5 Well, that is one of those scriptures that sounds great when you're not the one suffering, but Susan modeled the truth of Paul's words. She didn't blame God for what happened to her the day of her accident. She didn't blame God for her suffering. She wrestled with God for sure and she wondered about purpose and meaning but her faith in God was real, her hope in God's promises was real. Her love of Christ and surrender to His will was authentic.

The hope that never disappoints is not found in our will but in our surrender to the Holy Spirit who has poured out his love into our hearts! Susan epitomized what integrity and dignity is supposed to look like! She modeled forever what Paul meant in describing that we can still have joy in the midst of our suffering. But make no mistake, in my many conversations with Susan; this required some hard rock-pushing!

Susan was a class act and I am so glad that she was more than a congregation member, more than a saint of the church, more than fellow Christian, she was my friend and she taught me more about faith and hope and love and being a Christian than just about anyone else. My Lord, who could not love this woman? She would light up a room and even from her specialized wheelchair, she was still the tallest person in the room for her stature was one of divine origin, rising above the physical limitations she endured.

Susan was differently abled alright but never handicapped. Her abilities were extreme! She understood she was different after the accident and in some ways, better! At least that was how she looked at it; for she did not and would not be defined by her so-called limitations. Her abilities were extreme, before the accident and after!

- Her intelligence was extreme but was always displayed with humility.
- Her outward beauty was extreme but always displayed with modesty.
- Her inward beauty was extreme but always displayed with quiet assurance.

- Her spiritual gifts were extreme but always performed with gentleness.
- Her confidence was extreme but always manifested with unpretentiousness.
- Her strength was extreme but always tempered with caution.
- Her faith was extreme but always practiced with grace.

Susan pushed rocks her entire life. She pushed against rocks of injustice and oppression. She pushed against insufficient curriculum in our school system. She pushed against inadequate facilities. She pushed against any rock that attempted to hold children back. She pushed against rocks that were stifling young minds.

Let me share what a counselor wrote to me from one of the elementary schools Susan frequented as a guest.

"It is impossible to put into words the amazing impact she has had in the lives of children. Not only has she passed on her love of reading, and helped children to expand their horizons in the way they think about reading and literature, but she has also been an incredible role model and demonstrated in a most powerful way how a person can use their life, gifts, love, and talents and invest into the lives of others, no matter what barriers they may be facing. Her legacy will never be forgotten and the impact she has made in the lives of children will be felt forever! Thank you, Susan. You are truly one of God's precious gifts to us all and an inspirational example to follow! We will miss you."[2] Tiffany Markwood

Susan was able to push against the rock because she based her life and lived her life upon the rock of the Gospel. Friends, make no mistake about this. Susan was a devoted Christian.

When Susan shared her story and testimony at church, the main emphasis was not upon how she rose above her accident! It was not about how all the ways she remained strong. It was not about her momentary struggles and how she rose above them, it wasn't about her and what she did, it was about Him, and what He did! It was about the one who died on a cross for our forgiveness and who rose on the third day to give us the opportunity for eternal life. It was never about her; it was about Jesus!

She didn't know or understand why this accident happened just a little over two months after she married Barney. She didn't understand everything, but she was alright with God because she found a way like the serenity prayer says in, "Trusting that He will make things right if I surrender to His will; that I may be reasonably happy in this life, and supremely happy with Him forever in the next."[3] Reinhold Niebuhr

Susan, you don't have to push against the rock anymore! God has cleared the road; God has cleared the way and God has kept his promise.

I can see, in my mind's eye, Susan, dancing in heaven, dancing in a beautiful garden in the great outdoors, I can see her dancing with the Lord, I can see her standing, running, riding, teaching and basking in the sun light. I can see her with Jesus and with children all around her and with a few dogs running to her. I can see her, made new again and I can hear him, our Lord saying: "Well done good and faith servant!" Matthew 25:21

Let me close with this Psalm 116. If I didn't know better, I would have believed Susan had written it. "How can I repay the Lord for all his goodness to me? I will lift up the cup of salvation and call on the name of the Lord. I will fulfill my vows to the Lord in the presence of all his people. Precious in the sight of the Lord is the death of His saints. O Lord truly I am your servant and You have freed me from my chains. Psalm 116:12–16

One of the greatest gifts that can be given, one of the greatest of all seeds to share, is to model what suffering in faith and hope looks like for the believer. It is a holy undertaking!

Being cured and being healed is two different things. Susan may not have been cured, but she was most certainly healed. From the United Methodist book of worship, it says

God does not promise that we shall be spared suffering but does promise to be with us in our suffering. Trusting that promise, we are enabled to recognize God's sustaining presence in pain, sickness, injury, and estrangement. Likewise, God does not promise that we will be cured of all illnesses. The greatest healing of all is the reunion or reconciliation of a human being with God. When this happens, physical healing sometimes occurs, mental and emotional balance is often restored, spiritual health is enhanced, and relationships are healed. For the Christian, the basic purpose of spiritual healing is to renew and strengthen one's relationship with the living Christ.[4]

Let me say a word about Barney, who planted seeds of another variety but just as fruitful and conducive to a bountiful harvest.

Barney had the gift of mercy. This made him, for lack of a better word, a natural when it came to providing care. Can we imagine what it must have been like being married for only two months, after all he had gone through in his previous marriage, to once again find himself in the role of the caregiver? And to yet another overwhelming and demanding role?

Barney persevered through treatments, home renovations, daily procedures, hundreds of doctor visits, learning therapy techniques, watching for signs of depression, cooking, cleaning, and doing all this while holding down a job. Barney thrived in his role as caregiver and was an inspiration. If I am brutally honest with myself, I would like to think that I could stand up to the test if it became a reality in my family, but the truth is, I'm really not sure. I don't know how he was able to persevere. It would have so easy for him to cut and run. Why didn't he? I'll tell you why: faith, hope, and love!

Barney's surrender to Christ was total and without compromise. His love for his wife and the destiny that was set before him would be realized. For ten years, Barney fulfilled the painful and constant stress of the caregiver, and he did it with courage and devotion. He answered God's call for him to persevere. Barney inspired many people, and I dare say, he never knew it.

The seeds that Susan and Barney planted in my life will be with me, growing and sprouting forever. I cannot adequately express the depth of my profound and eternal gratitude for their faithfulness, perseverance, and hope. These are seeds, my friends, that will spring forth fruit one hundred times over! They are seeds worth considering.

"We need to remind ourselves that God can change things. Outlook determines outcome. If we see only the problems, we will be defeated; but if we see the possibilities in the problems, we can have victory."[5]

Quite often, people who mean well will inquire of me whether I ever ask myself, in the face of my diseases, "Why me?" I never do. If I ask, "Why me?" as I am assaulted by heart disease and AIDS, I ask, "Why me?" about my blessings, and question my right to enjoy them. The morning after I won Wimbledon in 1975, I should have asked, "Why me?" and doubted that I deserved the victory. If I didn't ask, "Why me?" after my victories, I cannot ask, Why me?" after setbacks and disasters. I also do not waste time pleading with God to make me well. I was brought up to believe that prayer is not to be invoked to ask God for things for oneself, or even for others. Rather, prayer is a medium through which I ask God to show God's will, and to give me strength to carry out that will. God's will alone matters, not my personal desires or needs. When I played tennis, I never prayed for victory in a match. I will not pray now to be cured of heart disease or AIDS. I do not brood on the prospect of dying soon. I am not afraid of death.[6]

Chapter 13

Seeds of Conviction
Jackie, "I've Found Christ!"

I was very fortunate to be raised by loving parents in a lower middle-class neighborhood during the sixties and seventies. Our streets were safe places where everyone knew everyone. I made money mowing yards in the summer and shoveling snow in the winter. We had the best sandlot in a ten-block radius where we played football in the fall and baseball in the summer. We challenged each other on who could ride a wheely the longest. It always came down to me and a kid named Marty. If you don't know what a wheely is, I feel sorry for you.

We had two mom-and-pop stores available to us where you could get anything you needed. They both had those wonderful soda pop coolers where you would slide the top open, feel the rush of cool air, and gaze down upon every flavor of soda imaginable. And they were all in bottles! Oh, what bliss! For a quarter, you could get a bottle of Crème Soda and a Fifth Avenue candy bar, or perhaps some wax lips or a pack of baseball cards. We attached the cards with a couple of clothespins to the spokes of our bicycle wheels to make them sound like they had motors! I cringe now when I think of how many Micky Mantle rookie cards I ruined in the spokes of my spider bike with the tiger grips and sissy bar. Again, if you don't know what they are, I'm sorry.

My dad used to send me to the closest store to get his cigarettes. We called that store "the Old Bags" for the cantankerous shopkeeper who owned the place. One time, when I was eight years old and was sent to buy my dad's Lucky Strikes, she grabbed me by the hand and said, "When your daddy comes in here, I'm going to ask him if he got all his cigarettes. You understand me, boy?" She was a scary woman who ruled her store with fear! She earned and deserved her name, or at least that is what we kids believed. But she had the best candy selection in town! She would really get mad when we would wear our cleats in her store after a Little League baseball game. She made us take our cleats off. Can you imagine that in today's world?

When school was out, we draped an old paint cloth over the clothesline in my backyard for our summer sleepovers. We had the city park right up the street less than a block from my house, and on a hot summer evening, it was a race between us kids to see who could nail down the batboy job for one of the fast-pitch softball teams. If you didn't get there in time, then you could always go out to the manual score board and hang up the metal numbers for the runs scored each inning.

If I did something to get into trouble, my parents knew it before I got home. I had a lot of freedom growing up, and I think it is because I was the last child, the baby of the family. My sister Libby was ten years older, and my brother Tim was four years older. I believe my mom and dad figured out that most of the things they feared was not going to happen and that almost all the things they worried about was not worth it. In other words, I had it made!

Those were good days for me. We were not rich; but we always had enough to pay our bills, have food on the table, clothes on our backs, and a roof over our head. We always had a great Christmas. We went to church, came home when the lights came on, sneaked rides on the back of the ice cream truck, rode our bikes everywhere, learned to deal with bullies, and learned to deal with getting picked last for the team.

We went barefoot in the summer, played in the dirt, drank out of the garden hose, picked strawberries from the orchard that was up the street beside the park, and simply reveled in our innocence. I had a wonderful and blessed childhood. I was far from a perfect kid, but I did know right from wrong, at least most of the time. I had good friends and was considered a good friend. I was an average, normal, well-adjusted, funny, athletic kid who was loved and nurtured by my parents and extended family, and that is what makes what I am about to share that much more bewildering. It would be oh so freeing to say the devil made me do it or I wasn't in my right mind or it was peer pressure. I guess it could be that all of those things played a part. The truth is I knew what I was going to do was wrong, but I did it anyway.

I was fourteen and a proud owner of a Kawasaki 100 cc motorcycle. There were about ten of us who were able to work, save, beg, borrow, and steal enough to get a motorcycle. Several blocks away for our neighborhood, where the streets turned to gravel and where fields were still wild, there was a string of old, abandoned, shale pits. This place was perfect for off-road motorcycle adventures! The place was always known by the odd name of the dinky. Now I never knew why or how it got its name; but the dinky, for adolescent motorcycle riders, was heaven on earth! I truly believe that when I get to heaven, I will be riding motorcycles again with my friends at the dinky.

Well, to this day, I don't know why I did it. I have tried to rationalize it, I have tried to analyze it, I have agonized over it, and I have suffered because of it. Looking back on it, I can blame no one but me, myself, and I! Please believe me when I say this was not the kind of kid I was, but nonetheless, I did what I did.

There was a kid named Jackie who would ride with us sometimes. Nobody liked Jackie, and I especially didn't like him because he had the same identical motorcycle I had. Jackie never really did anything to anyone. He did smoke pot and drink way before any of the rest of us gave those things a try, but he was not a tough guy or someone who was intimidating. He just had a way of getting on my nerves.

Jackie was very poor. You could tell by his clothes and his ragged appearance. No one knew for sure, but we all believed that Jackie's mother had either died or left and that Jackie's alcoholic father was trying to raise him. But we really didn't know any facts. One thing was sure, Jackie had a way of aggravating us.

Maybe it was the way he was always trying to become one of our group or maybe it was the way he rode. The truth is, we were cruel to Jackie, cruel to a boy who didn't have what all the rest of us had. I was cruel, there is no way around it, to a boy who needed a friend. I was cruel to a kid who just wanted to belong. We didn't have to go home to what Jackie had to endure. We all had secure homes with loving parents. Jackie went home to a filthy house, a negligent father, no mother, no money, and drugs.

So this church-going young man, who had it made, who was very lucky and enormously blessed in many ways, decided one day that he had had enough of Jackie and didn't want him around any longer. I was going to make him pay just for being who he was. I made a stupid decision that day. There was no excuse for my actions that day; and to add an extra measure of guilt, as I said before, I knew what I was doing was wrong and not what God would like but did it anyway!

In front of everybody, I told Jackie he had to pass a trust test if he wanted to hang with us. I told him if he wanted to ride with us, he had to pass this test. I told him he had to put his hands behind his back, close his eyes, and turn his head. I said, "I'm not going to hit you. You need to trust me. If you want to be in this club, you have to go through with this." Well, to my surprise, in his willingness to belong, he agreed to do everything I asked.

In his mind, he must have been thinking, *Finally, I'm going to belong and have friends.* Well at this point, I hauled off and hit him in the mouth as hard as I could and told him to not come back. Everyone laughed and said, "It had to be done." I was convicted immediately of my wrongdoing, and this would haunt me for a long time. In fact, to some degree, it still does.

When I got home that day, I was sick about what I had done. I knew it was wrong, but guess what? I didn't do anything about it. Sure enough, Jackie got the message, and he never rode with us again. In fact, I think he sold his bike. I never saw Jackie much after that. I'm not sure; I think he dropped out of school a few years later.

I moved on, but what I did plagued my conscience off and on for the next twenty years of my life. I was not a bully, and it was not in my character to do what I did to poor Jackie that day. I wish I could have gone back and chosen another direction. I had never been that kind of kid, and I decided I would never be that kind of kid again. But I never told Jackie I was wrong and I never apologized. I asked the Lord to forgive me, but I never asked Jackie. Fourteen or not, I should have done the right thing. Flash forward those twenty years, and you will see how God works in such serendipitous ways.

My son was ten years old and decided he wanted to play Little League basketball, so I became the assistant coach. Tryouts had already occurred; and the head coach, my friend Wayne, had picked the players and received the roster. The first day of practice came, and guess who showed up?

It has been twenty years; but Jackie looked the same, except he was well groomed, better dressed, and carried himself with confidence. He was personable and pleasant, and the love he had for his son was evident and wonderful to witness. There he was, after all this time, bringing his son to practice on my team. God has a sense of humor and an uncanny sense of justice!

We acknowledged each other with a certain amount of awkwardness but without any sense of animosity. It was, as if, neither one of us wanted to go back to that time at the dinky. We entered into the cliché niceties of placid and meaningless small talk. One day, our conversation became a little deeper, and Jackie told me that he had found Christ. He told me he found a great church and turned his life over to Jesus. He was excited to tell me that his relationship with Jesus had turned his life around. That the church had made all the difference in his life. He was drug free, working hard, and was happy and doing well. He said he had made peace with his past. All I could muster in this conversation was a lame, "Hey, I'm a Christian too." Pitiful.

I knew from day one of practice that God had orchestrated this serendipitous reunion, and I was even more convicted as to what I needed to do. It was only a question of when and where. I was convicted by God of my wrongdoing twenty years ago and was once again reconvicted by God of what I needed to do now! I needed to apologize and ask for forgiveness.

Well, the season was almost over, and I had finally mustered up the courage to go through with my plan. I would do it soon, but not today. A couple of weeks went by, and the season ended and I still had not stepped up to the foul line. It was a few days later that I opened the newspaper to see Jackie's name in the obituaries. I found out later that Jackie had a heart ailment that went undiagnosed for years. He suffered a massive heart attack in his early thirties and died instantly.

Was God teaching me? Was God convicting me? Was God telling me that I was "hearing but never understanding" and that I was "seeing but not perceiving"? (Matthew 13:14).

Was God telling me that "my heart was calloused"? (Matthew 13:15). The answer to all of these questions was yes. God did not orchestrate these events to teach me, but God certainly took these events and presented me the lamentation of missed opportunity! God was not scolding me or berating me. God was convicting me! There is a difference. God's correction is always with love. It is always positive. It is always grace filled. Oh, make no mistake—there is accountability but never shaming.

Conviction is positive. It is God casting seed on difficult soil in hope that the hard path, the weed, or rocky soil will be cultivated into fertile ground! God loves me and there is nothing I can do to make God not love me; but God will still compassionately hold me accountable by gently, and sometimes not so gently, reminding me of opportunities I have missed or ignored, opportunities to be a positive influence for the kingdom here on earth and opportunities to repent.

Was Jackie permanently affected by my bullying that fateful day? I will never know in this side of heaven, but I do know I missed several opportunities to be the face of Jesus and willfully decided to be disobedient to the Holy Spirit. Jackie overcame; and he was happy and involved in the church and was giving witness to anyone who would open their ears, eyes, and hearts to the good news! Seeds of conviction are painful, but perhaps they are the seeds that are the most needed sometimes.

I know this: if I am riding motorcycles in heaven at the good old dinky, I hope Jackie will be there and I hope he has forgiven me. I have made peace with my conviction, and I praise God that He loved me enough to place within my spirit seeds of self-examination and repentance. I'm sorry, Jackie!

These are difficult seeds but seeds worthy of consideration.

"Conviction is worthless unless it is converted into conduct."[1]

"The nearer Christ comes to a heart, the more it becomes conscious of its guilt; it will then either ask for his mercy and find peace, or else it will turn against Him because it is not yet ready to give up its sinfulness."[2]

"The son said to him, 'Father, I have sinned against heaven and against you. I am no longer worthy to be called your son.'

"But the father said to his servants, 'Quick! Bring the best robe and put it on him. Put a ring on his finger and sandals on his feet. Bring the fattened calf and kill it. Let's have a feast and celebrate. For this son of mine was dead and is alive again; he was lost and is found'" (Luke 15: 21–24)

Chapter 14

Seeds of Service
Linda, Lunch Lady of Love

In 1994, the great *Saturday Night Live* comedians Adam Sandler and Chris Farley preformed a tribute sketch about the public-school lunch lady. I say it was a tribute sketch because they didn't so much make fun of the cliché lunch lady image as they, in their special comedic creativity, honored her. It was very funny and at the same time poignant.[1]

My mother-in-law, after working most of her life as a waitress and convenience store clerk, found her niche as a middle-school lunch lady. The cards we received when she died in 2013 filled several boxes, and all of them shared stories of what a profound influence this lunch lady had upon their lives. Oh, it wasn't that she had made a great financial donation to the school or started a protest for some injustice. It wasn't that she was fighting for equality or better wages or better food for our children. What instigated such an outpouring of love was the truth of her genuine affection, concern, and love for others, especially children.

Whether it was her smile, the pride she took in her job, or the fact that she spoke to everyone with joy in her heart, the truth is, people responded to her service. My mother-in-law was passionate about her job and believed rightly so—that she, in her own small way, was making a difference in people's lives.

Children who came through her lunch line never went hungry because they didn't have money. No child, under her watch, would suffer extreme embarrassment because they forgot their lunch money or let their school account become depleted or were just plain poor. Many times, Linda would very quietly cover their costs with her own money. This was especially significant and worthy of admiration in that she was not a wealthy person.

My in-laws were not poverty ridden but certainly could not afford to take care of others' financial issues. It is fair to say that they always, as long as I knew them, struggled with finances.

My mother-in-law had a great need to serve others, and I believe this was her gift and her passion. She was not happy unless she could be helping someone or doing those behind-the-scenes tasks that no one else wanted to do. She loved to cook for her family, and she loved to babysit for her grandchildren and great-grandchildren. During the holidays—when everyone else was playing board games, talking, or watching a football game—she would be the one in the kitchen doing the dishes. She did this because she loved to do it, just like she loved to greet the children that came through her lunch line. She knew all of their names and always greeted them with a smile. Even teachers and administrators loved to visit with this lunch lady of love.

Now don't think for one minute that my mother-in-law was meek and mild. She was a loving woman who wanted and even needed to serve, but she could be meaner than a junkyard dog and more protective than a grizzly bear mama with cubs when it came to her children and grandchildren. On one occasion when she was watching my two boys, I guess they were about six and eight, she came home from a short excursion and discovered their bicycles, which had been parked on our carport, had apparently been stolen. Well, she remembered two boys on bikes going across a vacant field not too far from our house as they were coming back home.

Well, friends, she jumped in her car, and around the corner she flew and she caught up with those two boys who had indeed stolen her grandchildren's bikes. She cuffed them by the back of their necks, and needless to say, those boys were begging her to call the police just to get away from her wrath. Well, we didn't involve the police because I am quite sure by the time she got through with them, they would never steal bikes again!

My mother-in-law Linda never knew her mother. Nettie was her name, and she died at the age of twenty-eight from a heart attack. Linda was only two. She and her sister went to live with their maternal grandmother, a wonderful woman named Rosey.

Linda's father, Carl, had to work and relied on his mother-in-law to help raise his daughters. This arrangement worked well for several years. Eventually, her father remarried, and Linda's life took a difficult turn. At the age of eleven, she moved in with a stranger who made it abundantly clear that she married their father, not them. I will not dwell on this except to say the environment was so toxic that Linda wanted to get away from this proverbial wicked stepmother as soon as she could. And she did.

She met and married who would become the love of her life in 1957 at the age of sixteen, and a year later gave birth to her first of five daughters, who would become my wife! Linda had four children by the time she was twenty-one. She overcame many obstacles in her life. Her marriage was difficult for many reasons; but she was able, somehow, someway, to keep her family together and to raise five daughters who are all beautiful successful, compassionate, and caring people.

Those five daughters love each other very much and will always cherish their mother. They are still close. Each daughter had their own special memories of their mother; but all have become who they are today because no matter how difficult things were, no matter how challenging their lives could be at times, they knew that their mother loved them and would give her life for them.

I loved my mother-in-law very much and miss her. I miss her for selfish reasons because she was my biggest cheerleader. I could do no wrong when it came to Linda. She made me feel very special, but to tell you the truth, Linda always sought to see the best in people. Maybe her upbringing taught her to give people the benefit of the doubt. Maybe it taught her what pouring our grace to people really meant because she had experienced so little of it for most of her life.

I was especially moved when my mother-in-law, in 2007, decided to join the church. She had always believed in God but had not found a church home. I believe she never connected with a church because deep down inside her spirit, she never believed herself to be worthy. I assured her that if that were the case, none of us would be in church. Those seeds of unworthiness—and yes, shame—had been planted in her from a young age. Those seeds were from the evil one, and they took root until the day she turned her life over to Jesus.

She started attending Burnt Factory UMC, where I was serving, and really liked the people there. She was accepted, and it did wonders for a woman who struggled with self-esteem issues her entire life. I was so honored and so excited when she came to me and asked me to baptize her. It was a glorious day, and I will never forget baptizing my mother-in-law. She had found a church home and had truly found peace through Jesus Christ.

This lunch lady of love would come to need her Lord when in 2012, after what we thought would be a routine gallbladder surgery, she was diagnosed with bile duct cancer that had invaded her liver. It would be only seven weeks from diagnosis to death.

My mother-in-law faced this challenge with faith and blessed assurance, and she gave the family great inspiration as she exhibited peace in her heart throughout those seven weeks. She fought hard through chemo treatments that had no effect. Perhaps her greatest gift to her family, perhaps the most important seeds my mother-in-law sowed during this heart-wrenching time, were the seeds of courage.

She was not afraid to die; and although she did not desire to leave her daughters, who were also her best friends, she accepted that this was her cross to bear. She gave over her life to Jesus at her baptism. And now, she would enter into her new home, a home not made with human hands but eternal in heaven.

I was with mom when she took her last breath, and I thought what a wonderful God we worship that would grant our families such a wonderful mom! She may not have been the most educated, she may not have been the leading citizen of the town, she may not have had an easy life, and she may not have experienced all the bells and whistles of life. She suffered through evictions, electricity cut-offs, bill collectors, and living pay check to pay check. She suffered the loss of a baby boy who died at birth. She endured her husband's alcoholism, a terrible stepmother, and many more challenges. But she survived and survived with love and charity in her heart and with grace and forgiveness in her spirit.

The seeds she planted were rooted in finding fulfillment and purpose in serving others. Even in her death, she was serving others by showing her family how a person with faith claims the promise of the resurrection.

Linda, this lunch lady of love, could have chosen to be mean, resentful, spiteful, unforgiving, hateful, and ill-tempered. She could have quit on life a long time ago. She could have quit on her daughters, her husband, the world, life, and God! But she didn't, she didn't! She chose to live in love for her family; she chose to keep trying, to keep going, to find a way. She found contentment in the simple things of life.

Are these not valuable seeds that are worthy of cultivation in our soul soil? Are these not seeds worth considering?

"Love must be sincere. Hate what is evil; cling to what is good. Be devoted to one another in brotherly love. Honor one another above yourselves. Never be lacking in zeal, but keep your spiritual fervor, serving the Lord. Be joyful in hope, patient in affliction, faithful in prayer. Share with Gods people who are in need. Practice hospitality" (Romans 12:9–13).

"Everyone can be great. Because everyone can serve. You don't have to have a college degree to serve. You don't have to make your subject and verb agree to serve. You don't have to know about Plato and Aristotle to serve. You don't have to know Einstein's theory of relativity to serve. You don't have to know the second theory of thermodynamics to serve. You only need a heart full of grace. A soul generated by love."[2]

Chapter 15

Seeds of Wisdom
The Last Thanksgiving—the Choice

In 1994, my wife and I were tasked with hosting our family's Thanksgiving celebration. Now my wonderful sister, Libby, had hosted this most-cherished family tradition annually for many, many years. She made everything so special and wonderful. Her table and preparations were always impeccable, and all the family would gather with such gratitude and warmth. Her home in North Carolina was comfortable and accommodating and filled with love. Unfortunately, the fall of 1994 presented some difficulties that required a different approach because my father and brother were ill and unable to travel to North Carolina. My brother lived in New York City, and he was able to make it to Virginia where my father and my family still resided. But Dad just couldn't leave home.

To this day, as sick as my brother was, I don't know how he was able to get on a plane. I think he knew as we did, even though it was unspoken, that this would be his and my father's last Thanksgiving, and most likely the last time we would be together. What drove him was a great need to be home one last time.

My dad was seventy-two and suffering from esophageal cancer, and my brother was forty and suffering from AIDS. That last Thanksgiving was a simple celebration that garnered a deep and sincere appreciation for each other and all that God had blessed us with as a family. There were many hidden tears being shed behind closed doors.

It was one of those times when Jesus revealed his presence to me with such clarity. Jesus comforted me that day and would be my constant companion and friend in the difficult days that were on the horizon for my family; for I knew without a doubt that my best friend in the entire world, my father, did not have long to live on this earth. I also knew with certainty that my one and only brother, a gifted surgeon and brilliant scholar, was also not long for this old world.

As challenging as the coming days were going to be for me and my sister, I became acutely aware of how agonizing they were going to be for my mother. I was going to suffer the loss of my brother and father, but she was going to suffer the loss of her husband and son. She was going to have to endure being a member of that terrible club of parents who were tasked with burying a child. As hard as these losses were going to be for me, I cannot imagine what they would be for my mother.

My mother would be a beacon of strength during this time. She would give evidence of her faith by the way she nursed and cared for her beloved husband, and by the way she would—with honesty, integrity, compassion, and grace—deal with the loss of her son.

As I already shared in chapter 9, my mother processed the gift of mercy, but the gift of wisdom was also manifested in her spirit. This gift is not centered in knowledge as much as its foundation is built upon an intimate understanding of God's Word. It is given evidence in a person by upright and holy living. It is further exemplified through recognizing and discerning, in humility, decision-making that is grounded in the leading of the Holy Spirit. In other words, believers with this gift usually make the right decisions when they need to, and especially when those decisions are not easy.

Thanksgiving came and went, and my brother returned to New York where he was very much loved by many and where he received wonderful care. My dad continued to fight cancer the best he could with my mother doing the lion's share of caregiving.

This gift of wisdom would prove to be agonizingly painful for my mother as the diseases that were ravishing her husband and son would progress rapidly at the same time.

A few weeks after Thanksgiving, we received word that my brother Tim was declining, so mom and I jumped on a plane and made our way to St. Vincent's Hospital in New York. Tim happened to be the head of the surgery department at St. Vincent's. My sister came to be with dad.

The best way I can describe what we experienced is to share this. There is a scene at the very end of the groundbreaking movie *Philadelphia* where Tom Hanks's character, a lawyer, who is dying of AIDS, is in a hospital bed saying goodbye one by one to his family. It is a heart-wrenching scene. His character is on oxygen, fighting for each breath. His head is hairless from all the treatments. He is so weak, speaking is difficult. He still possesses his senses, and his brilliant brain is still working. The love he has for his family is vividly realized in his eyes. He is not angry, he is not afraid, he is not fighting; he is ready to surrender.[1]

This is exactly the scene that was played out when mom and I arrived at the hospital. When we said our goodbyes, with mom holding back the majority of her tears until we got outside, I looked back one last time because I knew I would never see Tim alive again.

Christmas came and went, and the first week of 1995 came to our family like a tornado. Tim's condition was dire; his death was imminent. At the same time, my father's condition worsened, and his life was hanging on by the thinnest of threads.

Here is where the strength of my mother shone forth and where she came to a crossroads that no one, especially no mother, should come to.

"Do I go to my son and abandon my husband at his greatest time of need or do I stay with my husband and abandon my son on his death bed?" Can we comprehend the choice?

Mom decided that her husband needed her most, and it was decided that my wonderful and compassionate sister would go to be with our brother.

My sister Libby was with Tim when he died, and he was comforted and at peace. Tim died on January 5, 1995. My father rallied and was able to come home from the hospital. He was able, with great help, to attend his son's funeral. Because of a snowstorm, the family could not attend the memorial service they held for Tim in New York City, but many of his friends and colleagues were able to travel to Virginia the following week for his hometown service of death and resurrection.

We would return to that same sanctuary at First United Methodist Church in just under three months as my father would claim the promise of the resurrection on March 25, 1995.

My mother's choice was a difficult one but I believe to be the right one. Her wisdom and discernment came from above; and even though she struggled with her decision, as anyone would, she eventually came to understand the terrible and unique situation as something she would need to endure. She suffered through 1995, and she did endure. And she eventually was healed. She persevered and held on to her Lord, her family, her friends, and her faith.

She got up each day, got dressed, put one foot in front of the other, and survived! "And the God of all grace, who called you to his eternal glory in Christ, after you have suffered a little while, will himself restore you and make you strong, firm and steadfast" (1 Peter 5:10).

The seeds of wisdom and courage that my mother, Edna, planted in our family in that defining year were seeds worth cherishing.

Our faith, when push comes to shove, is about making a choice.

My mother made a choice, and she endured because that's what believers do. We trust God and we persevere, sometimes by one agonizing step at a time.

As hard as 1995 was for my family, it was also a year of tremendous spiritual growth. I have found that I have not grown very much as a Christian in times spent on the mountaintop. I love the mountaintops of life, and it does solidify my humility and gratitude. I would stay on the mountaintop if I could; but it is in the valley, especially the valley of the shadow of death, where I have grown the most in my faith walk. It is there, in the midst of heartbreak and suffering, that I have experienced the compassionate presence of my Lord in such abundance. It is in the valley, where I need my Lord the most, that Jesus confirms everything I have ever believed about him! He does wrap his arms around us, he does cry with us, he does walk with us, and he does understand!

Romans 5:1–5 are difficult verses, and one needs to be careful and tender when deciding when to cite them. Having said that, I have found them, after some healing has taken place, to be true.

"Therefore, since we have been justified through faith, we have peace with God through our Lord Jesus Christ, through whom we have gained access by faith into this grace in which we now stand. And we rejoice in the hope of the glory of God. Not only so, but we also rejoice in our sufferings, because we know that suffering produces perseverance; perseverance, character; and character, hope. And hope does not disappoint us, because God has poured out his love into our hearts by the Holy Spirit, whom he has given us" (Romans 5:1–5).

The seeds my mother have planted in my life are bearing much fruit, not because of anything I have done but by what God has done through me and through the seeds my mother scattered and helped to cultivate in my life. Seeds of courage and wisdom are important seeds! Are they not worth considering?

My mother's choice was the right one for all the right reasons, and as painful as it was, it was born of deep faith and trust in God and in his Son, our Savior Jesus Christ.

"My hope is found in nothing less than Jesus' blood and righteousness. I dare not trust the sweetest frame, but wholly lean on Jesus' name. On Christ the solid rock I stand, all other ground is sinking sand, all other ground is sinking sand."[2]

"Courage is not having the strength to go on; it is going on when you don't have the strength."[3]

My mother made difficult choices as death loomed for her husband and son. She must have felt like a kindred spirit to the psalmist that wrote, "I am worn out from groaning; all night long I flood my bed with weeping and drench my couch with tears" (Psalm 6:6).

What I experienced in my mother's choice and in her continued faith, the seeds that were scattered my way are best summed up by Rabbi Steve Leder in his book *More Beautiful Than Before* where he writes, concerning death and our ability to move forward, these words of truth.

> "There is nothing I can say to make this easier. Death is an awful part of life. This is one of those times when you just put one foot in front of the other until it's over. Just keep going. That is all you can do and that is all you must do. 'I just can't' is sometimes the response."
>
> "You can and you will because you must," I tell them.[4]
>
> My mother and many others like her have just kept putting one foot in front of the other. They have endured because of the love and grace of God. When you must, you can!

Chapter 16

Seeds of a Sixth-Grader Named Sam—What Makes You a Winner

This school year has been a different year for me. I am in the sixth grade and my friends from the fifth grade are in different classes. Now, I have to make new friends and that was very difficult for me because I am a shy and quiet person. I was determined to do well this year. My goal was to make the honor roll. I have worked very hard to achieve good grades. So far this year, I have made the honor roll every time. Last year, I did not make the honor roll at all.

This has been a sad school year for a twelve-year-old. I have lost my uncle to AIDS in January of 1995 and my grandfather to cancer in March of 1995. My grandfather was my dad's best friend and mine. I wonder if you know the feeling of losing your best friend. My faith and determination has helped me through these deaths.

I have learned that hard work and attending school every day is the key to making your dreams happen. I have also learned that carting about other people is important because that is the way God wants us to be. A winner, for me, is a person who gives effort to whatever they want to do, whether it is at school or in daily living. I feel I am a winner because I have faith and a great family and I am a happy person.[1]

"Blessed are those who mourn, for they will be comforted. Blessed are the meek, for they will inherit the earth. Blessed are those who hunger and thirst for righteousness, for they will be filled. Blessed are the merciful, for they will be shown mercy. Blessed are the pure in heart, for they will see God" (Matthew 5:4–8).

Hard work, faith, family, and determination leads to a happy life. Perhaps, these are seeds worth considering.

I found my son Sam's letter one day as I was looking back through some of my grown children's memory storage boxes.

It was a letter he wrote for school in response to dealing with the death of two beloved family members.

We must never discount or fail to see the wonderful seeds of faith that are planted by our younger family members and friends.

When my four-year-old granddaughter, Abby, became enthralled with my friend Sonny's leg amputation, she was not shy about making inquiry. She was curious about his wheelchair and very curious about the fact that he had only one leg. She had been giving him the once-over for some time before she got her courage up and just walked right over to him, and in her beautiful innocence said, "What happened to your leg?"

Well, the usually somewhat gruff Sonny was enamored with her boldness and sweet charm. He said, "Well, honey, I lost it."

Abby, without hesitation, said, "It's okay. We'll find it." From that day on, Sonny was smitten and made sure Abby got chewing gum every Sunday!

Seeds planted by the most innocence among us can be seeds that get us through dark times and encourage us for the future.

Seeds planted by our youngest and most vulnerable can bring us hope like no other. These are seeds worth considering!

Jesus said, "Let the little children come to me, and do not hinder them, for the kingdom of heaven belongs to such as these" (Matthew 19:14).

Epilogue

There was a woman once who wanted peace in the world and peace in her heart, but she was very frustrated. The world seemed to be falling apart, and her personal life wasn't that great either.

One day she decided to go shopping, and she went to the mall and walked in to one of the stores. She was surprised to see Jesus behind the counter. She knew it was Jesus because he looked just like the paintings she'd seen in churches and in devotional books.

Finally she got up her nerve and asked, "Excuse me, but are you Jesus?"

"I am."

"Do you work here?"

"In a way; I own the store."

"Oh, what do you sell here?"

"Just about everything, feel free to walk up and down the aisles, make a list, see what it is you want, and then come back and I'll see what I can do for you."

Well, she did just that. She walked up and down the aisles, writing furiously. There was peace on earth, no more war, no hunger or poverty. There was peace in families, harmony, no dissension, no more drugs.

By the time she got back to the counter, she had a long list. Jesus looked over the list, then smiled at her and said, "No problem." And then he bent down behind the counter and picked out all sorts of things, and finally stood up, and laid out the packets on the counter.

"What are these?" the woman asked.

"Seed packets," Jesus answered. "This is a catalog store."

"You mean I don't get the finished product?"

"No, this is a place of dreams. You come and see what it looks like, and I give you the seeds. You go home and plant the seeds. You water them and nurture them and help them to grow, and someday someone else reaps the benefits."

"Oh," she said. "And she left the store without buying anything."[1]

The seeds of the faithful planted with love into our hearts give us roots and fruits.

The seeds of the faithful planted with sacrifice help us to desire to cultivate hard, rocky, and weed-infested soil.

The seeds of the faithful planted with humility provide grace that is prevenient, justifying, and sanctifying. These seeds can bring us to salvation, they can nurture us along the journey, and they can lead others to a decision.

The seeds of faith, offered in gratitude, can be passed on for generations.

The seeds of faith can strengthen and expand what defines family and what family means.

The seeds of faith can be embraced or ignored. They can be valued or tossed aside. They can be identified as vital and essential or regulated to peripheral.

The seeds of faith can be a revelation or aggravation.

The seeds of faith can be kept in secret or dispersed.

The seeds of faith planted with love, mercy, and grace can be a wellspring of wisdom.

The seeds of faith bring hope.

The seeds of faith are sown everywhere under difficult conditions because God's Word can penetrate through adversity. God's word can overcome any obstacle. The seed is the beginning and renewal of life.

The seeds of the faithful, the seeds of God, can be received or ignored. We can buy the seed or we can walk out of the store empty-handed. The choice will always be ours and the benefit to the kingdom of God on earth will be in the balance.

The mission statement of the United Methodist Church is "to make disciples of Jesus Christ for the transformation of the world."[2] We can achieve this only by choosing to cultivate a victory garden! We do it by establishing roots that cannot be torn out, scattered, and snatched away by the evil one. We do it by not allowing culture, with its many temptations, to take our focus off tending to the seed and the fruit. We can achieve a victory garden by standing firm through adversity. Planting roots that go through and beyond the rocky places, roots that go around the weeds. We do it by choosing to believe and trust in God!

"But the seed falling on good soil refers to someone who hears the word and understands it. This is the one who produces a crop, yielding a hundred, sixty or thirty times what was sown" (Matthew 13:23).

The Word of God, both written and living in Christ Jesus, is the truth behind the victory garden. It is the only way to establish the harvest.

> I am the true vine, and my Father is the gardener. He cuts off every branch in me that bears no fruit, while every branch that does bear fruit, he prunes so that it will be even more fruitful. You are already clean because of the word I have spoken to you. Remain in me, as I also remain in you. No branch can bear fruit by itself; it must remain in the vine. Neither can you bear fruit unless you remain in me. "I am the vine; you are the branches. If you remain in me and I in you,

you will bear much fruit; apart from me you can do nothing. If you do not remain in me, you are like a branch that is thrown away and withers; such branches are picked up, thrown into the fire and burned. If you remain in me and my words remain in you, ask whatever you wish, and it will be done for you. This is to my Father's glory, that you bear much fruit, showing yourselves to be my disciples. (John 15:1–8)

"My food," said Jesus, "is to do the will of him who sent me and to finish his work. Don't you have a saying, 'It's still four months until harvest'? I tell you, open your eyes and look at the fields! They are ripe for harvest" (John 4:34–35).

The seed that is the word of God, the seed that is Jesus, the seed that is revelation, the seed that is truth will only benefit the Kingdom of God here on earth and will only benefit the receiver of the seed if we choose to allow it to penetrate our lives. Fruitfulness is the goal of this wonderful parable. An abundant harvest is the goal of every seed.

Friends, we may never experience the bountiful harvest of the seeds of faith we share with others. We may not ever, in this side of heaven, receive verification of transformed lives. The good news is that we don't need to. It is enough that we receive the seed with gratitude and humility. It is enough that we receive the seed and share it with others.

God and only God knows what harvest will come. As the wonderful Natalie Sleeth hymn "Hymn of Promise" affirms.

"In the bulb there is a flower; in the seed an apple tree; in cocoons, a hidden promise: butterflies will soon be free! In the cold and snow of winter there's a spring that waits to be, unrevealed until its season, something God alone can see."[3]

Friends, one day, the seed that is our earthly body will be planted for all eternity. But that seed will produce, through the grace and promises of God, a new creation.

"The body that is sown is perishable, it is raised imperishable, it is sown in dishonor, it is raised in glory; it is sown in weakness, it is raised in power; it is sown a natural body, it is raised a spiritual body" (1 Corinthians 15:42–44).

My prayer and hope for this book is that the seed of God's Word will be desired with great zeal. I pray that the seeds of the faithful, scattered and sown in love through the power of the Holy Spirit, will be recognized, appreciated, cherished, and shared. I pray that this book in some modest way will perhaps enlighten a deeper understanding and appreciation for all those seed scatterers in our life.

I pray that we who claim Christ as our Lord will with confidence and humility join the ranks of the farmers of God, and that victory gardens will be plowed, nurtured, and loved. I pray that these gardens will flourish for the glory of God; and yes, that they produce a crop, yielding a hundred, sixty, or thirty times what was sown!

"Praise God, from whom all blessings flow; praise him, all creatures here below; praise him above, ye heavenly hosts; praise Father, Son, and Holy Ghost. Amen"[4]

Study Questions

Chapter 1

Steve suggests that some seeds of the faithful may be inherited. That legacy seeds from the past may have an influence on our present. In no way does this mean we are destined to be who and what our ancestors were; but it does mean that perhaps, through the Holy Spirit, we do benefit spiritually by those who have gone before us.

1. Do you have family legacies that have had an influence on your life of faith? And if so, have those influences been positive or negative? How so?
2. Have you heard stories of your ancestors? Have they had a part to play in your spiritual formation?
3. Steve references what has been coined as the love chapter from 1 Corinthians 13. Is there a difference biblically between charity and love? How does this chapter speak to Christian practice?
4. Radical hospitality is a theme in this chapter. What is the nature of hospitality for the faithful in today's culture?

Chapter 2

Steve suggests that there can be joy in the midst of struggle and that attitude has a huge part to play in how a person survives catastrophic life changes.

1. Have you known people who have not just overcome calamitous accidents but who have done so with great joy? What seeds of faith have they planted?
2. What role does acceptance of your destiny play in establishing your spiritual formation?
3. How important is attitude toward healing? How important is it in scattering seeds of faith to others?
4. How important is the role of caregiver? Have you filled that role? Have you supplied that role?
5. How does the quote from Mel Walker speak to you?
6. Is the passage from James difficult? How so?

Chapter 3

Steve suggests that patience is one of the greatest of gifts. Especially the patience involved in listening. In today's fast-paced world, taking the time to listen to someone who desperately needs to be heard is a rarity to say the least.

1. Have you experienced times when you needed to be a great listener? How was that experience? Was it difficult? Did your mind wander? Were you in a hurry?
2. Sometimes, we need to *be* in the moment. Do you find it difficult to just *be* there for someone without offering comment or solutions or advice?
3. How does the quote from John Wesley challenge you?
4. How do we place Galatians 6:9–10 into practice in today's world?

Chapter 4

Steve suggests that trusting God is the cornerstone to our faith. Especially trusting God in our darkest hours. Trusting God does not mean we don't question why. Trusting God does not mean we don't get angry with God. Trusting God does not mean we celebrate devastating illness, accidents, oppression, and injustice. Trusting God does not mean we give up. Trusting God does mean that there will come a time, a day, a season, when we need to surrender to God's will. We do not, so much, give up as we give over.

1. Have you experienced seeds of faith scattered upon your soul by those who have faced death with great faith and trust? If so, did it strengthen your faith? Did it advance your discipleship?
2. Why is the Book of Lamentations in the bible? The passage quoted in this chapter is one of the few positive passages in this book. Is it helpful? How so?
3. How do you navigate the unfairness of life? What does God's word say about it?

Chapter 5

Steve suggests that one of the greatest acts of kindness is to act with compassion beyond the given standard. Kindness can sometimes create risk and vulnerability. What is the given standard?

1. Was the decision to grant the dying man, in this context, a last wish, going too far?
2. Have you experienced situations in your life that have formed and perhaps tainted your perspective on what kindness means and how to apply it?
3. Does kindness have limitations? Does this chapter challenge you? What would you have done?

Chapter 6

Steve based this book on his first mission experience to a third-world country. He suggests that stepping out of comfort zones can pave the way for fruitfulness. His trip to Haiti in 2010 changed his life and perspective. The nurturing and love he received by mentors and friends helped to cultivate some suspect soil in his soul.

1. When was the last time you stepped out of your box and experienced something new? Was it a good experience?
2. How does 1 Timothy 6:17–19 speak to you?
3. Is mission a part of your Christian experience and practice? If so, share.
4. Steve used two sermons to best express his experiences in Haiti. Did they encourage you to seek out new opportunities and experiences to be in service to our Lord? How did the stories Steve shared in these sermons speak to you? Have you had experiences you would like to share?
5. Compare the quotes of John Wesley and Robert Louis Stevenson in this chapter with Hebrews 13:15–16. Discuss how these challenge or work in your life of faith.
6. Define goodness. Is God always good? Is goodness God's nature?

Chapter 7

Steve suggests that peace can be obtained through simplicity and that contentment breeds peace. He suggests that paying attention to the little things of life can have a profound influence on your peace.

1. Steve suggests that peace could be a choice. Do you agree?
2. How does Philippians 4:11–13 help us understand peace?
3. Steve says he still struggles with finding peace daily. How about you?

4. What can we do to make peace a more permanent part of our spirit?
5. Does the prayer of St. Francis help?
6. How important is fellowship and friendship to your peace?
7. How important is the beauty of creation to finding peace?

Chapter 8

Steve suggests that gentleness can be found in our relationship to our pets. That gentleness is manifested in unconditional love.

1. Have pets been a part of your joy in this life? Share.
2. How do we learn about gentleness from our pets?
3. Can you recall and share a story from the gospels when Jesus modeled gentleness?
4. What did you think of Rev. Billy Graham's quote?

Chapter 9

Steve suggests that mercy can be defined as a gift of the Holy Spirit that manifests itself in good works and in compassionate service to others, especially in the area of caregiving.

1. Could this gift be passed down? Could it be hereditary or taught?
2. How does Matthew 25:31–46 speak to you?
3. Have you had to provide care for someone? Have you needed care? Share how you felt in both giving and receiving help.
4. Is honoring your mother and father a difficult commandment? How do we honor a parent that has not been all they could have been?
5. How does the passage from 2 Corinthians 1:3–4 speak to you?
6. How does Jesus, being the prince of peace, influence our decision making?

Chapter 10

Steve suggests that teaching is more than a job. He infers that it is a calling.

1. Do you agree? Have you had similar experiences with teachers, both from Sunday school and public school?
2. Share good and bad experiences and how you dealt with it.
3. Who was your top-three favorite teachers?
4. Do you agree with James from chapter 3:1?

Chapter 11

Steve suggests that we are all human beings and most of us need encouragement at some time in our lives. It is not why we do what we do, but it sure helps cheer us on in this old world. It sure picks us up when we are down, and it sure helps us gain confidence and bread for the journey.

1. Share a time when someone encouraged you. Tell how it influenced you.
2. Has the truth of Joshua 1:9 helped you on your journey? Do you find encouragement from God's Word? From our Lord?
3. Why does encouragement seem to be such a difficult thing for us to give?
4. When did you encourage someone?
5. Which stories in the Bible are specifically encouraging to you? And why?
6. Steve quotes from "Amazing Grace." Are there other hymns or songs that inspire you?

Chapter 12

The story of pushing against the rock is an example of perseverance and obedience. Steve suggests that faithfulness in the face of devastating accidents and illnesses can have positive influences on healing.

1. Have you had experiences where endurance and faithful perseverance through difficult circumstances has helped you find peace and joy in the midst of the storm?
2. What is your understanding of Arthur Ashe's perspective on this topic? Do you agree with his assessment of prayer and of surrender?
3. Many times, the caregivers and other family members of those who have suffered difficult circumstances are forgotten. They can have very serious mental health issues as well as physical issues. How serious are we to take our marriage vows? Does God really want us to be devoted in sickness too?
4. Being healed and being cured are two different things. What is the difference?

Chapter 13

Steve suggests that the Holy Spirit helps to hold us accountable for our actions, and we have a choice. We can choose to act upon the leading of the Spirit or ignore and grieve the Spirit. When we ignore the Holy Spirit, we open ourselves to the lies of the evil one.

1. Do you agree with Steve that God's conviction of our wrongdoing is always done with compassion and positivity? If not, why not?
2. Do you think God desires to shame and ridicule us when we sin?
3. Why is forgiveness (granting and asking) so important to the Christian?
4. Does Fulton Sheen's quote resonate with you?
5. Have you ever been bullied? Have you ever been the bully? Looking back now, how has this affected your life?

6. Are we meant to live in shame and guilt? Look at Luke 15:11–32.

Chapter 14

Steve suggests that service to others is a gift that can set us free from the bondage of self. He suggests that service to others can grant a person direction, meaning, and purpose, even in the midst of a difficult life.

1. What part does service to others play in your life? What missions and ministries give you joy?
2. Does Matthew 25:31–45 help you understand service for the kingdom?
3. How does Dr. King's quote encourage you?
4. Have you known people who have overcome their circumstances through the joy of serving?
5. Can you think of passages in the Bible where a positive attitude is modeled?

Chapter 15

Steve suggests that every day, Christians are tasked with making choices. Some are trivial and some are life changing. Most are somewhere in between. The Holy Spirit will aid us in our decision-making, but that does not make certain decisions easy.

1. Have you grown spiritually more on the mountaintop or in the valley? Share.
2. Romans 5 suggests that we should rejoice in our sufferings. What does Paul mean?
3. We try and make choices based upon gathering pertinent information. We try and discern, pray, and meditate upon appropriate responses, but many times, emotions are raw. Many times, we have to make split decisions. We do the best we can and take peace in knowing that God knows our

struggle. Have you had to make similar decisions as found in this chapter?

4. How does Rabbi Steve Leder's quote challenge you?

Chapter 16

1. How has children influenced your discipleship?
2. What seeds have been scattered your way by children and youth?

Index of Scripture

Chapter 4
John 11:21–27
John 11
John 14:1–6
Lamentations 3:22–25
1 Thessalonians 1:3
Psalm 9:10

Chapter 5
Ephesians 4:32
Hebrews 4:15

Chapter 6
Psalm 91:1–6
Psalm 91:14–16
Psalm 27:1
1 Timothy 6:17–19
Psalm 91:14–16
2 Corinthians 5:7
1 John 1:6–7
John 3:16
Psalm 23 (KJV)
Mark 1:7
Matthew 14:27
Matthew 21:9
Luke 9:16–17
Matthew 19:14
Matthew 25:31–32
Matthew 26:75
Matthew 6:25–27
Matthew 6:33
Proverbs 31:10–31(Paraphrased)
Psalm 23 (KJV) (Paraphrased)
Hebrews 13:15–16

Chapter 7
Philippians 4:11–13
Hebrews 12:14

Chapter 8
Isaiah 11:6–7

Part 2
Romans 12:6–8

Chapter 9
2 Corinthians1:3–4
Exodus 20:12
Matthew 25:34–40

Chapter 10
Proverbs 17:22
Proverbs 15:13
Philippians 4:12–13
James 3:1
Colossians 3:13

Chapter 11
Matthew 6:22
Matthew 5:16
Hebrews 10:35
Joshua 1:9

Chapter 12
Romans 8:28
Ecclesiastes 9:11–12
Romans 5:3–5
Matthew 25:21
Psalm 116:12–16

Chapter 13
Matthew 13:14
Matthew 13:15
Luke 15: 21–24

Chapter 14
Romans 12:9–13

Chapter 15
2 Peter 5:10
Romans 5:1–5
Psalm 6:6

Chapter 16
Matthew 5 4–8
Matthew 19:14

Epilogue
Matthew 13:23
John 15:1–8
John 4:34–35
1 Corinthians 15:42–44

Endnotes

Preface
1. Robert H. Schuller, "Robert H. Schuller Quotes," AZQuotes. com, https://www.azquotes.com/quote/262278.
2. Jonathan Andersen, "The Myth of the 'Wesleyan Quadrilateral,'" *Jonathan Andersen* (blog), May 3, 2012, https://www.jonathanandersen.com/the-myth-of-the-wesleyan-quadrilateral.

Acknowledgments
1. *The United Methodist Hymnal* (The United Methodist Publishing House, 1989), 99.

Introduction
1. Pope Francis, "Pope Francis Quotes," BrainyQuote.com, https://www.brainyquote.com/quotes/pope_francis_571233.

Part 1
1. Joyce Meyer, "Joyce Meyer Quotes," BrainyQuote.com, https://www.brainyquote.com/quotes/joyce_meyer_567620.

Chapter 1
1. Tom Brokaw, *The Greatest Generation* (New York: Random House, 1998).
2. Maya Angelou, Quotes, Goodreads.com, https://www.goodreads.com/quotes/284542.

3. Shannon Alder, Quotes, Goodreads.com, https://www. goodreads.com/quotes/455308.

Chapter 2
1. *The United Methodist Hymnal* (The United Methodist Publishing House, 1989), 867.
2. Mel Walker, "What Is Joy in Christianity?" https:// www.christianity.com/wiki/christian-terms/what-is-joy-in-christianity.

Chapter 3
1. Yogi Berra, "Yogi Berra Quotes," BrainyQuote.com, https:// www.brainyquote.com/quotes/yogi_berra_135233.
2. John Wesley, *A Plain Account for Perfection* (Kansas City: Beacon Hill Press, 1966) https://www.worldinvisible.com/ library/wesley/8317/831711.htm.
3. Leo Buscaglia, Overallmotivation.com, https://www.over-allmotivation.com/quotes/leo-buscaglia-quotes.

Chapter 4
1. Paraphrase of Robert L. Lynn poem by Chuck Swindoll.
2. John 14: 1–6, paraphrased by author.
3. Robert L. Lynn, *Cancer Is So Limited and Other Poems of Faith* (Createspace Independent Pub, 2013).

Chapter 5
1. Steve Leder, *More Beautiful Than Before: How Suffering Transforms Us* (Hay House Inc., 2017), 59.

Chapter 6
1. Lowell D. Streiker, *An Encyclopedia of Humor* (Hendrickson Publishers, 1998), 271.
2. Christian Jokes, Facebook, https://www.facebook.com/ christianjokes1/posts/379758275477284.

3. John Wesley, Quotes, Goodreads.com, https://www. goodreads.com/quotes/12757-do-all-the-good-you-can-by-all-the-means.

4. Robert Louis Stevenson, Quotes, Goodreads.com, https:// www.brainyquote.com/quotes/robert_louis_stevenson_ 101230.

Chapter 7

1. Mother Teresa, "Mother Teresa Quotes," BrainyQuote.com, https://www.brainyquote.com/quotes/mother_teresa_ 107846.

2. "Prayer of St. Francis of Assisi," *The United Methodist Hymnal* (The United Methodist Publishing House, 1989), 481.

Chapter 8

1. *Baker Evangelical Dictionary of Biblical Theology* (Baker Books, 1996).

2. Rev. Billy Graham, "Billy Graham Quotes," AZQuotes. com, https://www.azquotes.com/quote/114841.

Part 2

1. Rick Warren, "Your Gifts and Talents Are Not Just for Your Good," *Daily Hope with Rick Warren*, Crosswalk.com, https://crosswalk.com/devotionals/daily-hope-with-rick-warren-january-9-2021.html.

Chapter 9

1. Eleanor Roosevelt, Quotes, BrainyQuote.com, https:// www.brainyquote.com/quotes/eleanor_roosevelt_121157.

2. Andy Stanley, "Andy Stanley Quotes," AZQuotes.com, https://www.azquotes.com/quote/811789.

3. George Washington, Quotes, Goodreads.com, https:// www.goodreads.com/quotes/24983.

Chapter 10
  1. Dalai Lama, "Dalai Lama Quotes," AZQuotes.com, https://www.azquotes.com/quote/531264.

Chapter 11
  1. Alexander MacLaren quote: www.christianquotes.info/quotes-by-author/alexander-maclaren-quotes/.
  2. *The United Methodist Hymnal,* (The United Methodist Publishing House, 1989), 378.

Chapter 12
  1. "The Unmoved Rock," Bible.org, https://www.bible.org/illustration/unmoved-rock.
  2. Tiffany Markwood quote used with permission.
  3. Reinhold Niebuhr, "The Serenity Prayer," Prayerfoundation.org, https://www.prayerfoundation.org/dailyoffice/serenity_prayer_full_version.htm.
  4. *The United Methodist Book of Worship* (The United Methodist Publishing House, 1992), 613–614.
  5. Warren Wiersbe quote: www.christianquotes.info/quotes-by-topic/quotes-about-change/.
  6. Arthur Ashe and Arnold Rampersad, *Days of Grace: A Memoir,* (University of California: Alfred A. Knopf, 1993), 290.

Chapter 13
  1. Thomas Carlyle, "Thomas Carlyle Quotes," BrainyQuote.com, https://www.brainyquote.com/quotes/thomas_carlyle_163811.
  2. Fulton J. Sheen, "Fulton J. Sheen Quotes," AZQuotes.com, https://www.azquotes.com/author/13447-Fulton_J_Sheen?p=3.

Chapter 14
1. Saturday Night Live, "Lunch Lady Land," posted September 26, 2013, YouTube.com, https://www.youtube.com/watch?v=VY14zcUM9SI.
2. Martin Luther King Jr., *The Words of Martin Luther King, Jr.* (New York: Newmarket Press, 1958), 17.

Chapter 15
1. Scene description from *Philadelphia* (1993).
2. *The United Methodist Hymnal,* (The United Methodist Publishing House, 1989), 368.
3. Theodore Roosevelt, "Theodore Roosevelt Quotes," AZQuotes.com, https://www.azquotes.com/quote/1055999.
4. Steve Leder, *More Beautiful Than Before: How Suffering Transforms Us* (Hay House Inc., 2017), 6.

Chapter 16
1. Sam Melester quote used with permission.

Epilogue
1. Brett Blair, *Collected Sermons*, https://www.sermons.com.
2. *United Methodist Book of Discipline* (The United Methodist Publishing House, 2016), 93.
3. *The United Methodist Hymnal,* (The United Methodist Publishing House, 1989), 707.
4. *The United Methodist Hymnal,* (The United Methodist Publishing House, 1989), 95.

About the Author

Steve Melester is the pastor at Burnt Factory United Methodist Church in Stephenson, Virginia, where he has served for sixteen years. Steve is a graduate of the Wesley Theological Seminary Course of Study program and is an associate member of the Virginia Annual Conference of the UMC. Steve worked in his family HVAC business for twenty-seven years before answering the call to full-time pastoral ministry in 2005. Steve lives in Winchester, Virginia, where he was born and raised, with his high school sweetheart and wife of forty-three years, Melanie.

CPSIA information can be obtained
at www.ICGtesting.com
Printed in the USA
BVHW080004211221
624507BV00006B/150